Page 21

1 2 3 4 5

Page 29

6 7 8 9 10

Page 36

I0801346

Page 45

BIG TRUCKS

Magnificent Monkeys

Amazing Ants

Pretty Princess

FAST CARS

I can practice holding a pencil correctly.

You need:

Let's practice using the **tripod grip**.

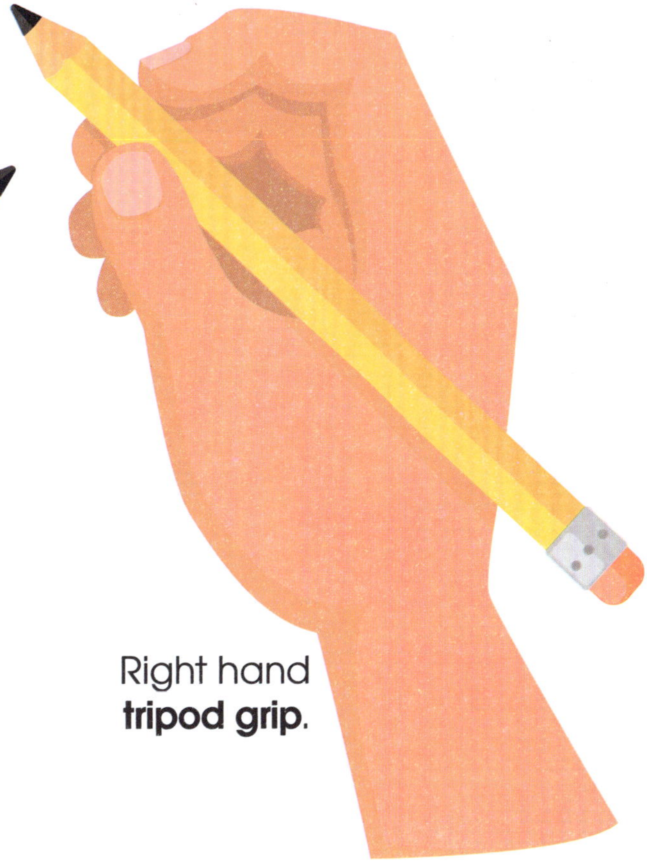

Right hand **tripod grip**.

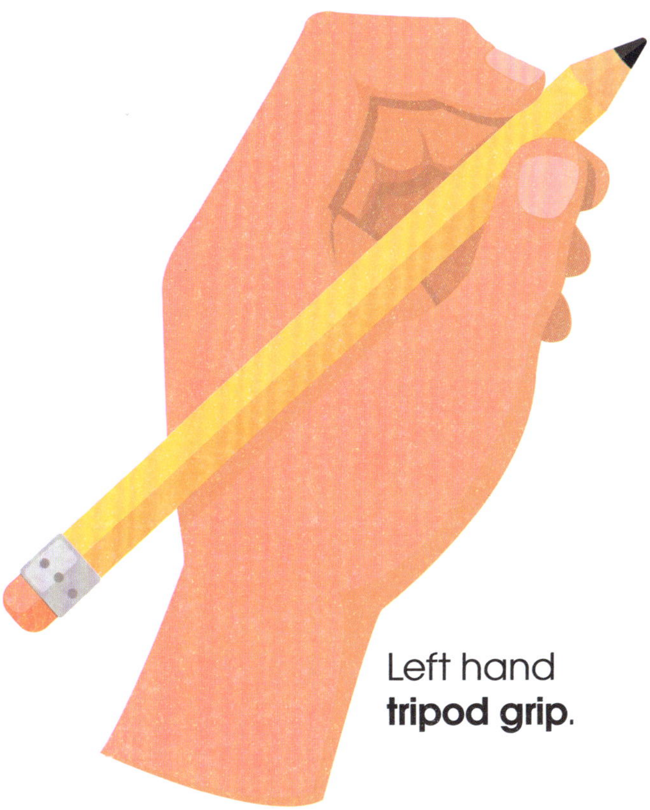

Left hand **tripod grip**.

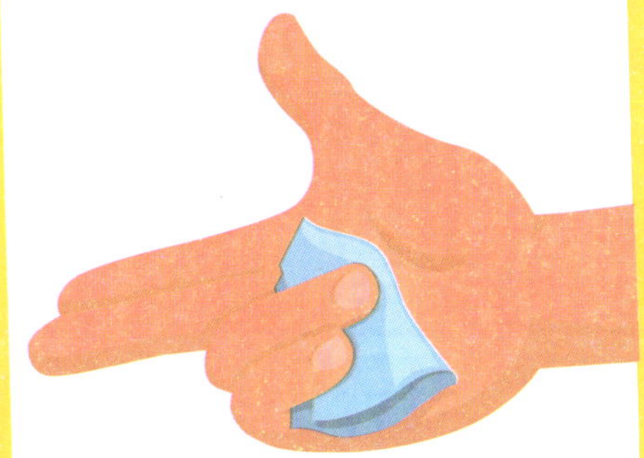

Parent Tip:
Don't pressure your child to use their left or right hand. Let them choose and encourage the proper grip. Put a tissue under the other two fingers for them to hold in place.

Online Extra:
To go to this activity, use your smartphone camera, hover over this code, and click on the link. Or go to: **anywhereteacher.com/qr/14161/01**.

I can trace lines.

Use the tripod grip!

Trace the **lines** from **left** to **right**.
Start at the red dot (●).

Got it!   Not yet

You need:

I can identify colors.

This  is green.

This  is purple.

Color the green.

Color the purple.

Got it! Not yet

You need:

I can identify colors.

These 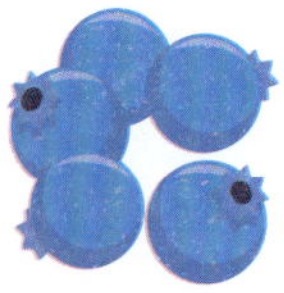 are blue.

This  is orange.

Parent Tip:
Even when using crayons or other writing utensils, encourage your child to use the **tripod grip**.

Color the orange.

Color the blue.

Got it! Not yet

I can trace lines.

You need:

Use the tripod grip!

Trace the **lines** from **top** to **bottom**.
Start at the red dot (●).

Practice drawing the **lines** from **top** to **bottom**.
Start at the red dot (●).

Trace the **lines** from **bottom** to **top**.
Start at the red dot (●).

Practice drawing the **lines** from **bottom** to **top**.
Start at the red dot (●).

Got it! Not yet

You need:

I can identify colors.

This is **brown**.

This is **pink**.

Color the **brown**.

Color the **pink**.

Got it! Not yet

You need:

I can identify colors.

This is red.

These are yellow.

Color the red.

Color the yellow.

Got it! Not yet

I can trace lines.

You need:

Use the tripod grip!

Trace the **lines** from **top** to **bottom**.
Start at the red dot (●).

Practice drawing the **lines** from **top** to **bottom**.
Start at the red dot (●).

Trace the **lines** from **bottom** to **top**
Start at the red dot (●).

Practice drawing the **lines** from **bottom** to **top**.
Start at the red dot (●).

Got it! Not yet

You need:

I can identify colors.

This  is **black**.

This  is **gray**.

This is **white**.

Color the **black**.

Color the **white**.

Color the **gray**.

Got it!   Not yet

You need:

I can trace lines.

Trace the **lines** starting at the **top**, curve around the **bottom**, and end at the **top**. Start at the red dot (●).

Practice drawing the **curved lines** starting from the **top**. Start at the red dot (●).

Trace the **circles** starting from the **top**. Start at the red dot (●).

Practice drawing the **circles** starting from the **top**. Start at the red dot (●).

Got it! Not yet

I can identify colors.

You need:

Color the pictures in each row that should be **green**.

Color the pictures in each row that should be **red**.

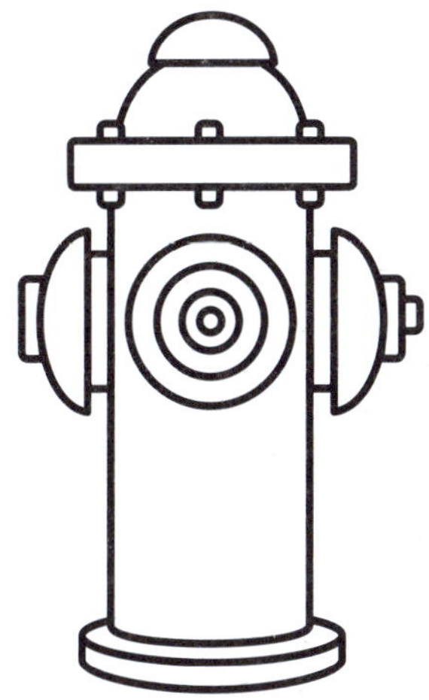

Color the pictures in each row that should be **purple**.

Got it! Not yet

You need:

I can identify colors.

Say the name of each food.
Color the food.

Parent Tip:
Visit AnywhereTeacher.com and search for **Colors, Shapes & More Flash Cards.**

Got it! Not yet

You need:

I can identify colors.

Color the picture.

Let's have some fun!

You need:

Help Socrates find his way home.

Draw a line from the owl to his house.

Got it!   Not yet

You need:

I can start to understand that a group of objects has a number word and a number.

0 zero

Circle the tree branch with **0** birds.

Got it! Not yet

You need:

I can start to understand that a group of objects has a number word and a number.

1 one

Trace 1 umbrella.

Got it! Not yet

You need:

I can start to understand that a group of objects has a number word and a number.

2 two

Trace 2 .

Got it! Not yet

You need:

I can start to understand that a group of objects has a number word and a number.

3 three

Trace **3** nails.

Got it! Not yet

You need:

I can start to understand that a group of objects has a number word and a number.

4 four

Trace 4 .

Got it! Not yet

You need:

I can start to understand that a group of objects has a number word and a number.

5 five

Color 5 balloons.

Got it! Not yet

I can start to understand that a group of objects has a number word and a number.

You need: 3

Count each group.

Find and place the stickers 3 for the matching numbers.

Parent Tip:
Have your child touch each picture as they count.

Got it! Not yet

I can count to 5.

You need:

Connect the dots from **1** to **5**.
Color the picture.

Got it! Not yet

I can count to 5.

You need:

Trace the path from **0** to **5**.

Got it! Not yet

You need:

I can start to understand that a group of objects has a number word and a number.

6 six

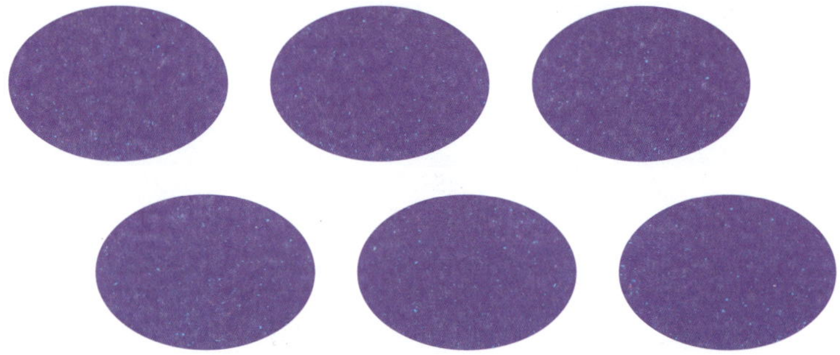

Trace 6 bones.

Got it! Not yet

You need:

I can start to understand that a group of objects has a number word and a number.

7 seven

Color 7 ☐.

Got it! Not yet

You need:

I can start to understand that a group of objects has a number word and a number.

8 eight

Trace 8 fish.

Got it! Not yet

You need:

I can start to understand that a group of objects has a number word and a number.

9 nine

Trace 9 ◇ on the snake.

Got it! Not yet

You need:

I can start to understand that a group of objects has a number word and a number.

10 ten

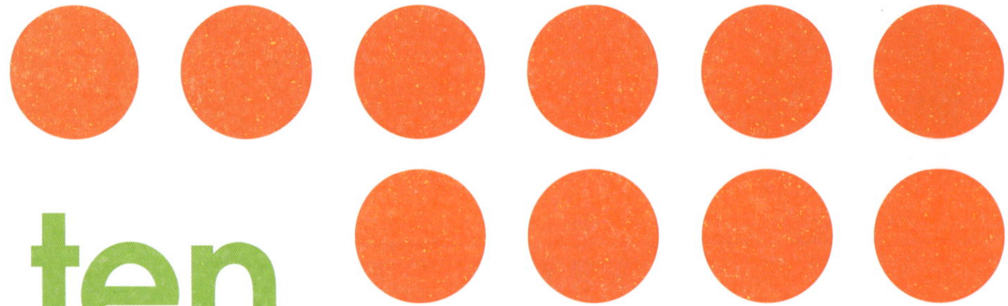

Trace **10** acorns.

Got it! Not yet

I can start to understand that a group of objects has a number word and a number.

You need: 8

Count each group.

Find and place the stickers 8 for the matching numbers.

Got it! Not yet

You need:

Let's have some fun!

Connect the dots from **1** to **10**.
Color the picture.

Got it! Not yet

I can sort shapes.

You need:

Spread out the press-out shape pieces in front of you.
Sort the shapes into the two groups below.

circle	not circle

Got it! Not yet

I can sort shapes.

You need:

Spread out the press-out shape pieces in front of you.
Sort the shapes into the two groups below.

square	not square

Got it! Not yet

I can sort shapes.

You need:

Spread out the press-out shape pieces in front of you.
Sort the shapes into the two groups below.

triangle	not triangle

Got it! Not yet

I can sort shapes.

You need:

Spread out the press-out shape pieces in front of you.
Sort the shapes into the two groups below.

rectangle	not rectangle

Got it! Not yet

I can sort shapes.

You need:

Spread out the press-out shape pieces in front of you.
Sort the shapes into the four groups below.

circle	square
triangle	rectangle

Got it! Not yet

I can match shapes and colors.

You need:

Look at each row.
Find and place the shape stickers that match each color.

Got it! Not yet

I can name common shapes.

You need:

Cut out the game boards on pages 37-42.
To play you need the spinner and crayons.

Directions:

Player 1 spins the spinner. Say the name of the shape and then color a matching shape on your game board.

Give the spinner to player 2 so they can spin and do the same.

If you spin the spinner and you have already colored in all of those shapes, do not color a shape and pass the spinner to the other player.

The player that colors all of the shapes on their game board **WINS**!

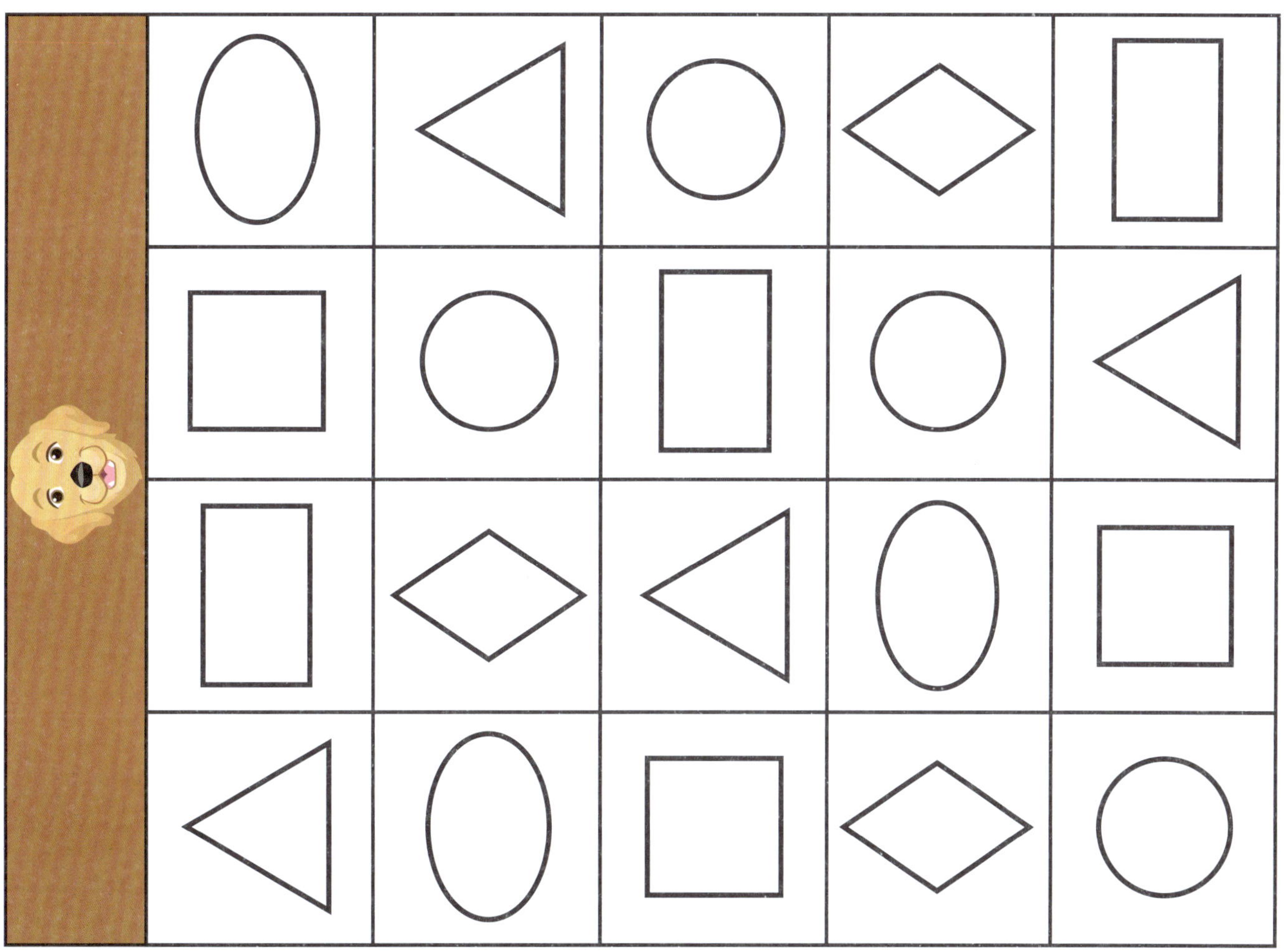

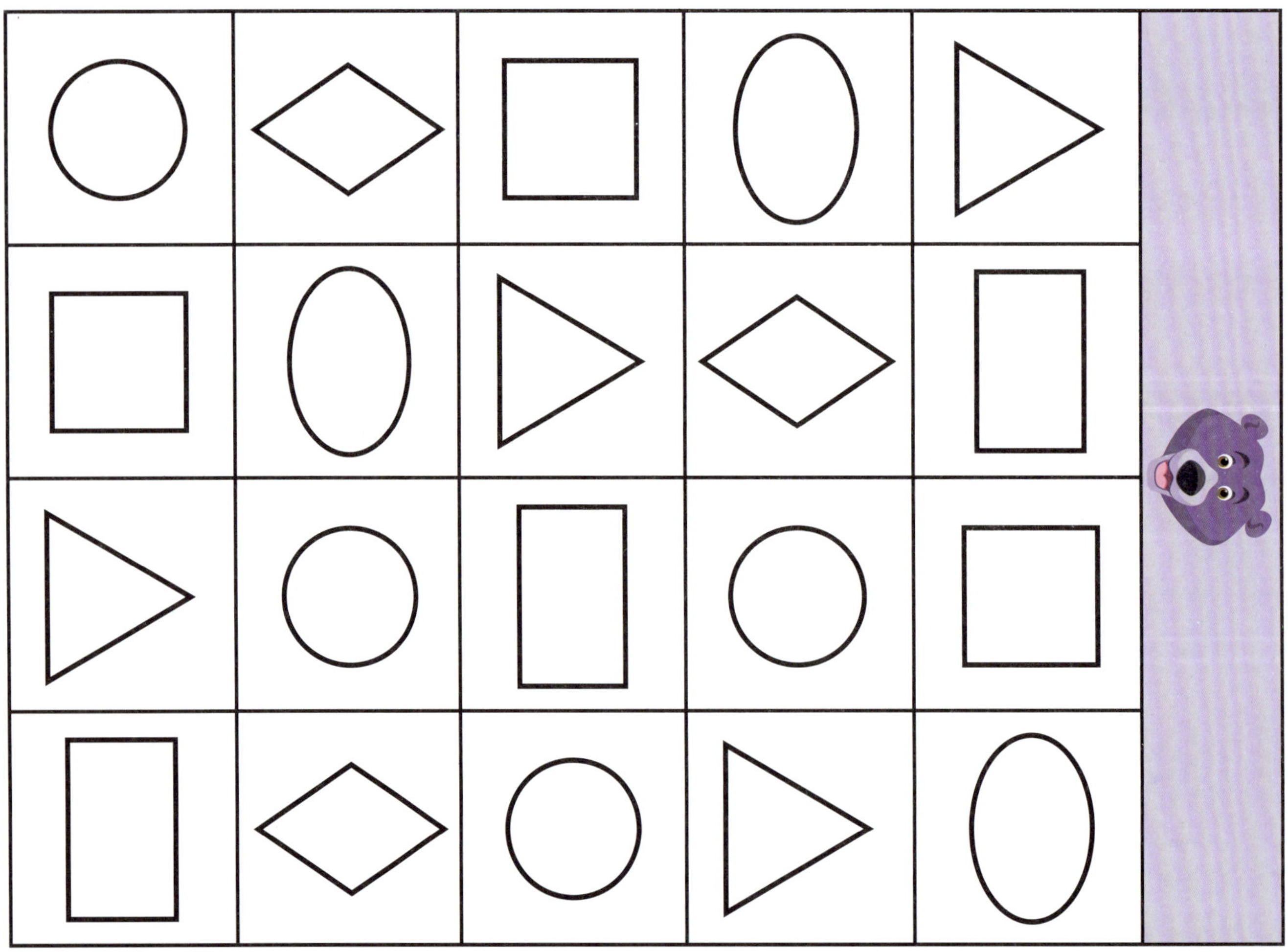

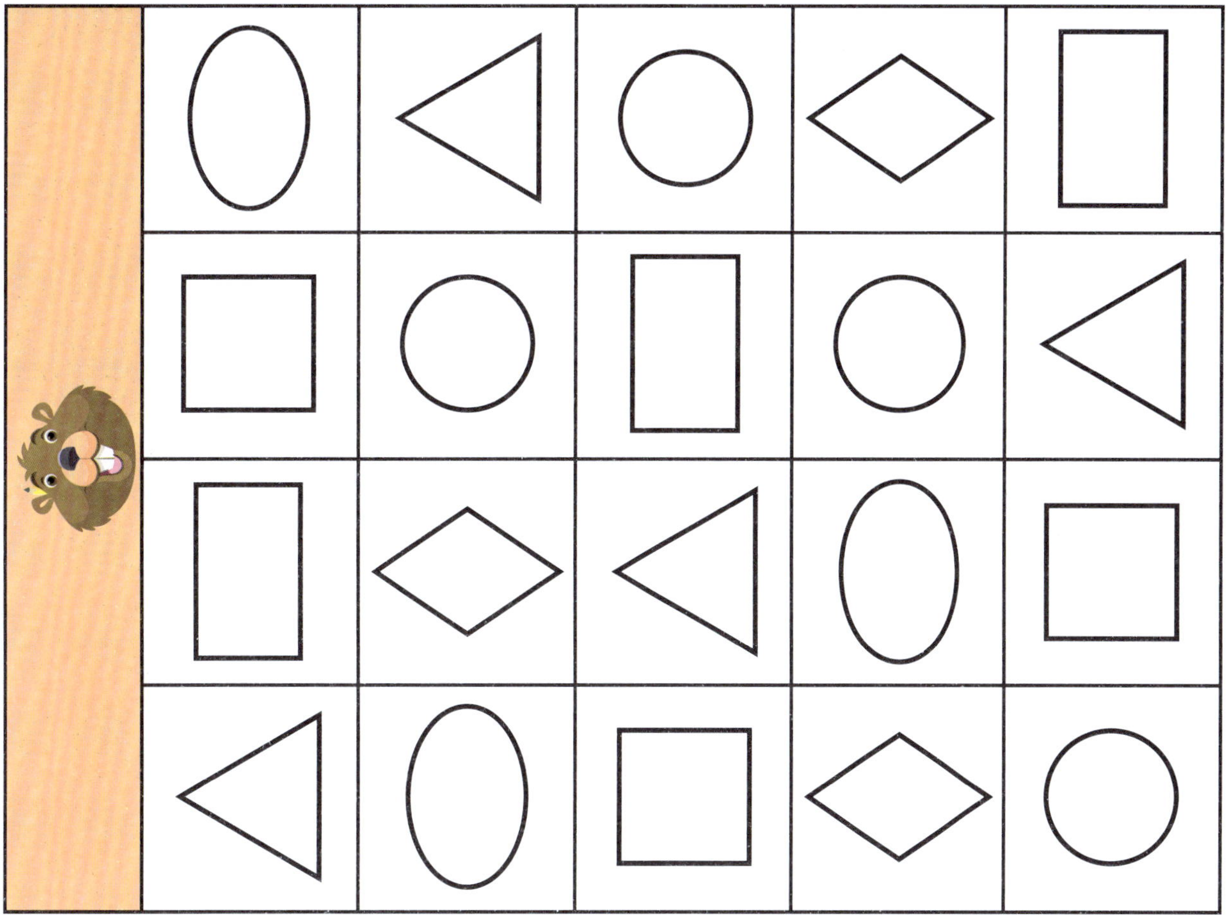

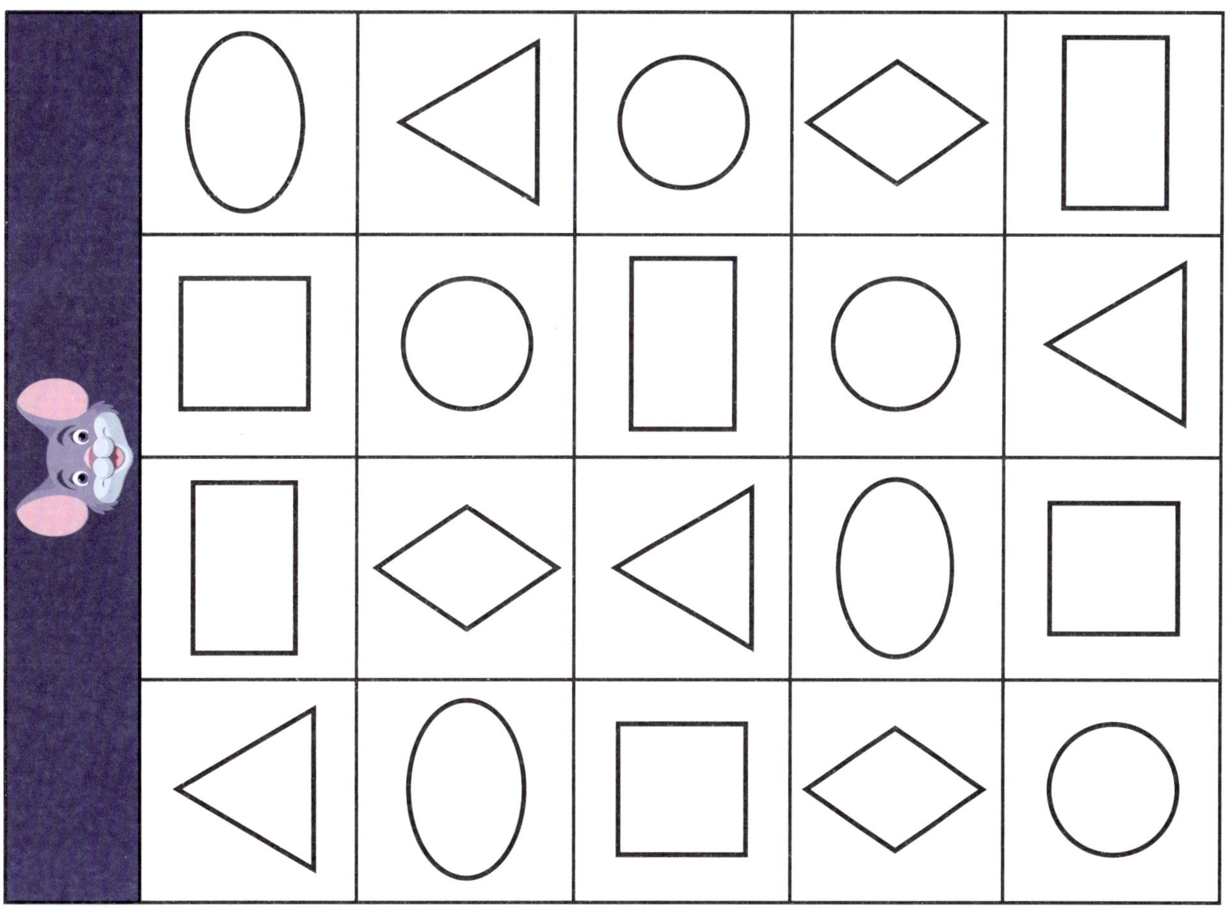

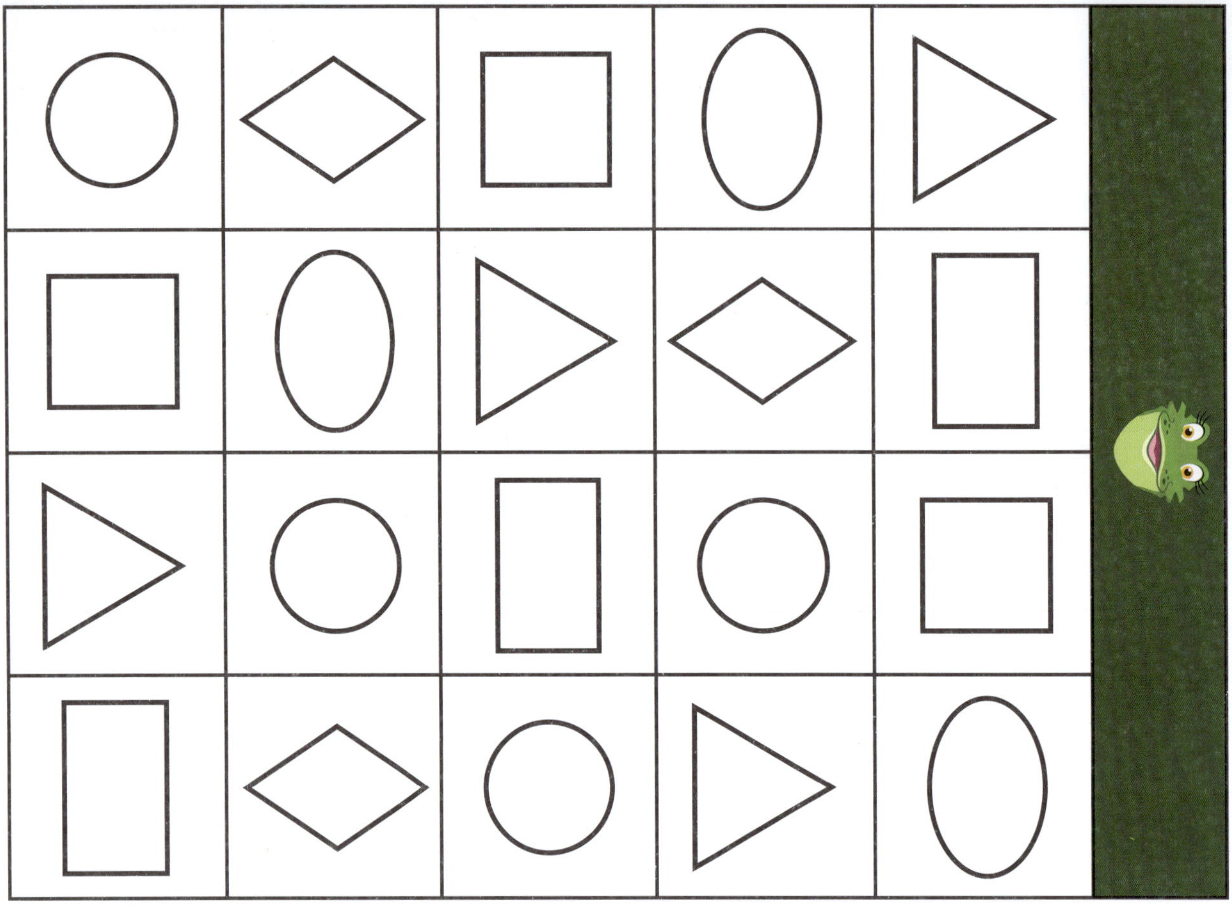

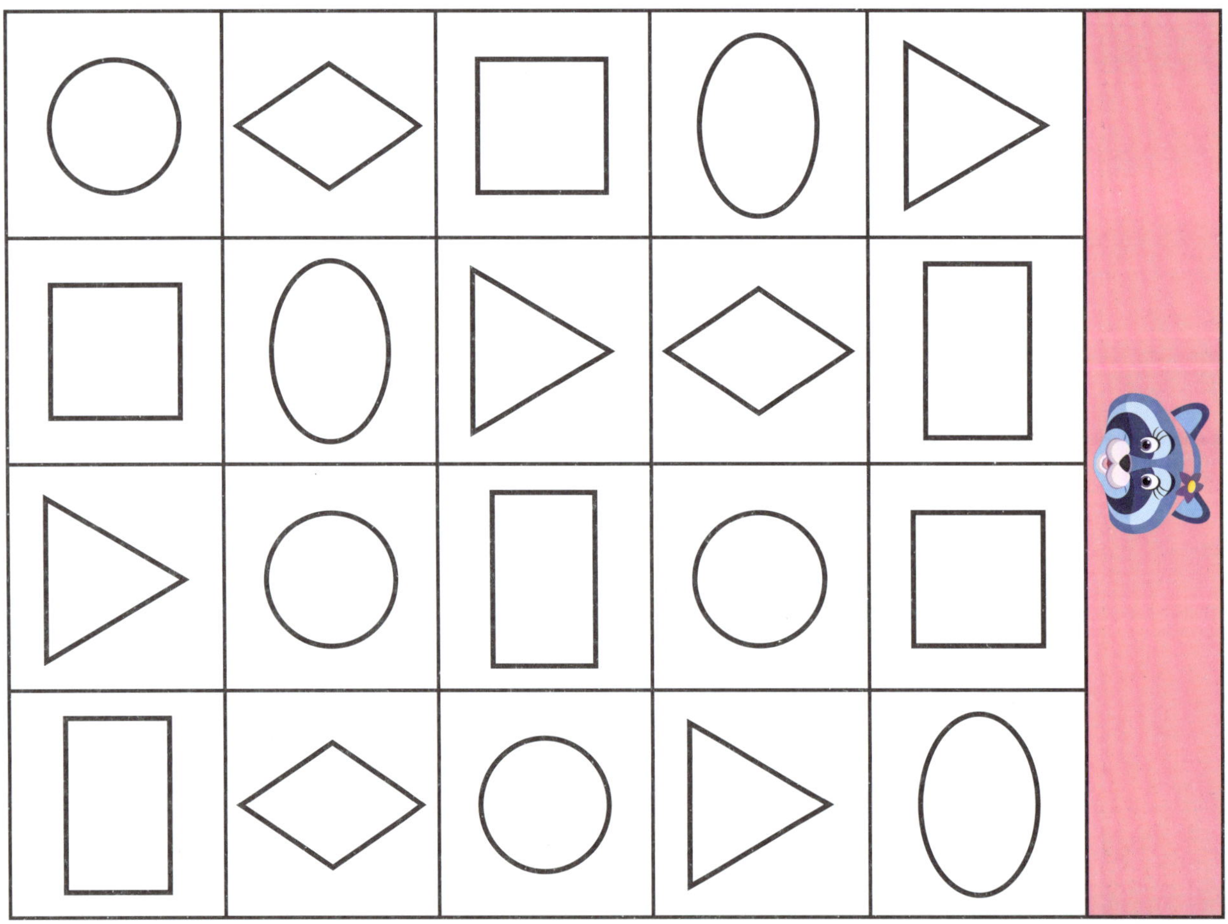

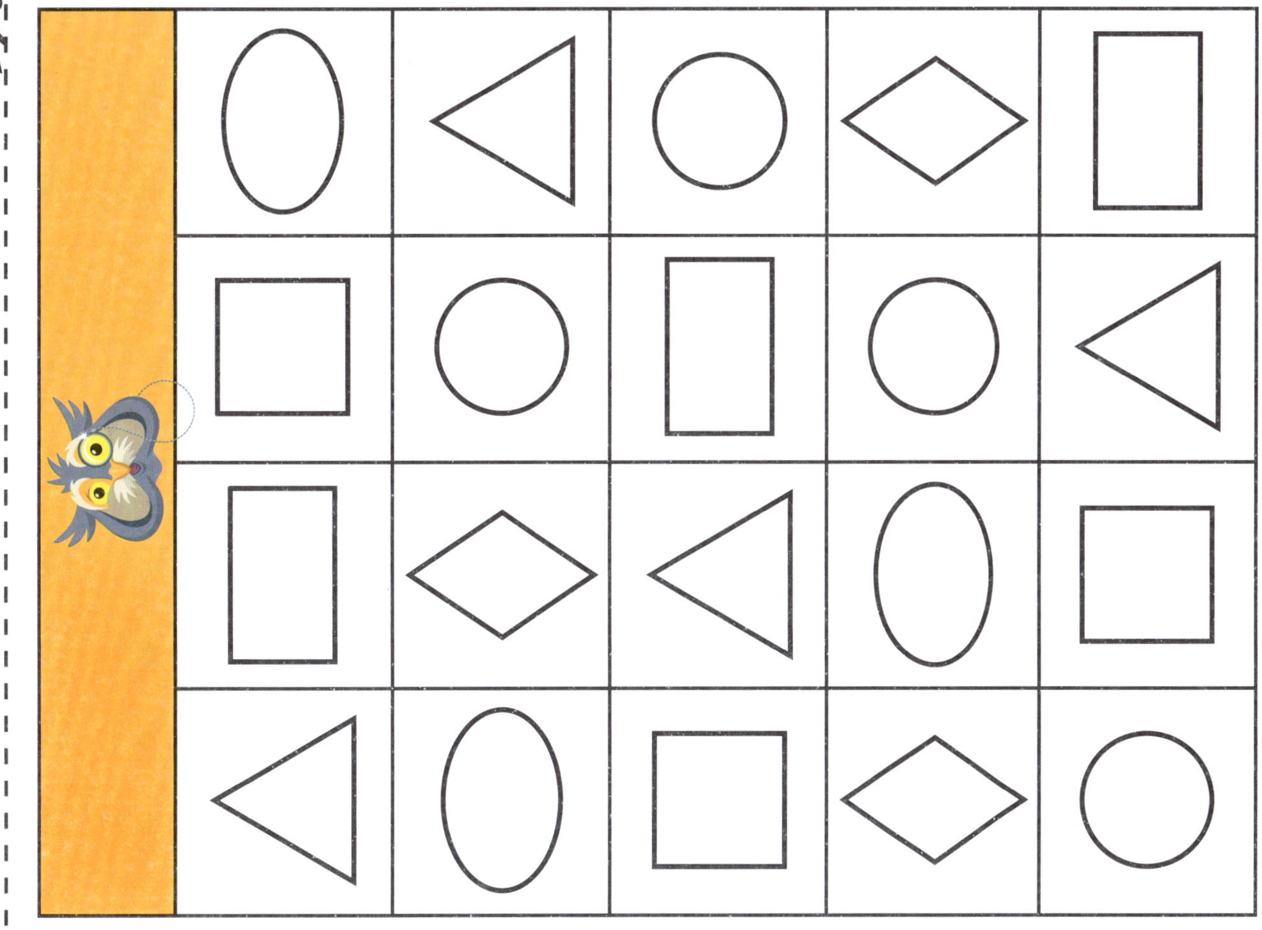

WANT MORE?

If you want to play more games, you can make your own boards. Draw a grid on a piece of paper and draw in the shapes you want in the boxes. Make sure you use all of the shapes you have learned!

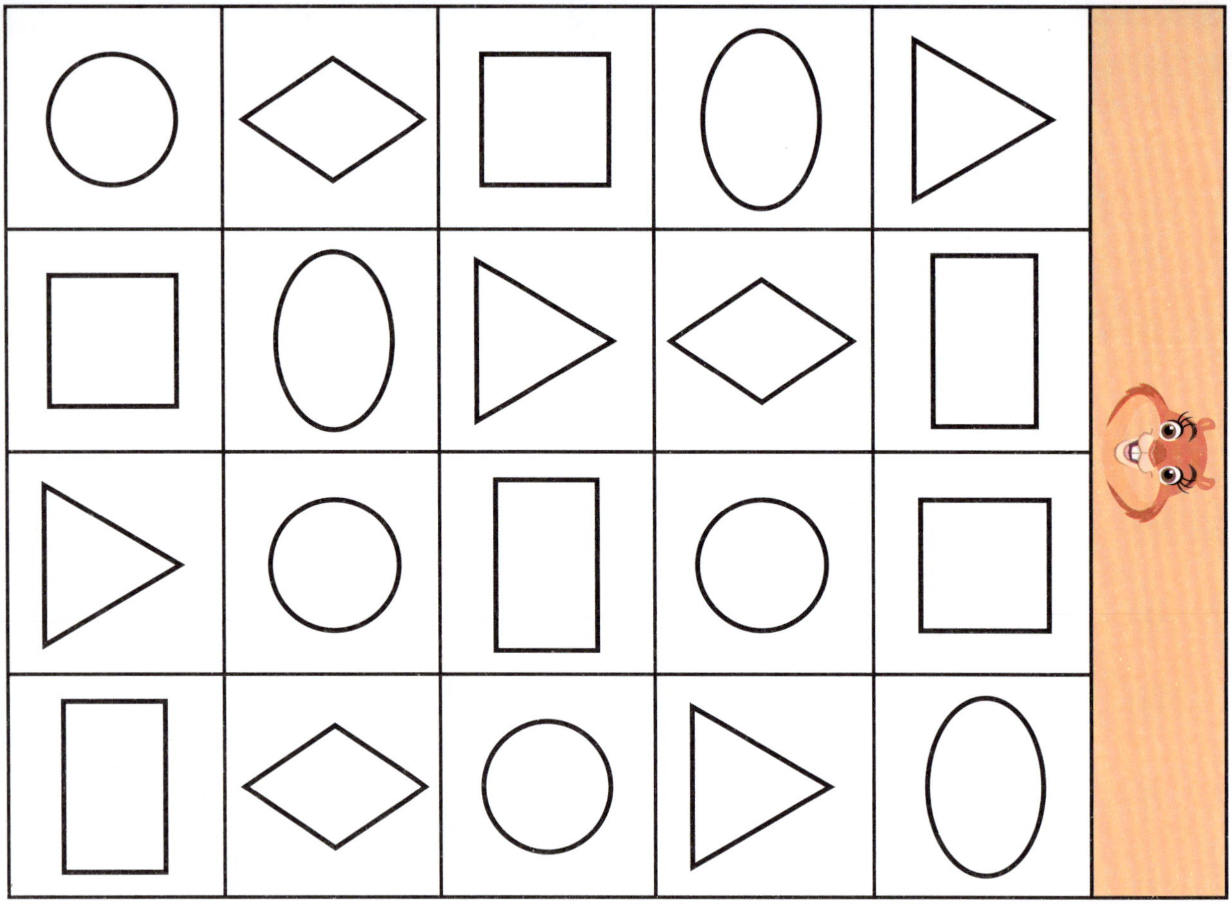

I can point to the cover, title, and back cover on a book.

Find a book in your house and point to the different parts.

Online Extra:
To go to this activity, use your smartphone camera, hover over this code, and click on the link. Or go to: **anywhereteacher.com/qr/14161/02**.

The **front cover** of a book has larger words and large pictures.

The **back cover** of a book usually has small words and smaller pictures.

The **spine** of a book usually has the title of the book on it.

Got it! Not yet

You need:

I can point to the cover, title, and back cover on a book.

The **title** is the name of the book.
The title is on the front cover in big letters.

Underline the title on each book.
The first one is done for you.

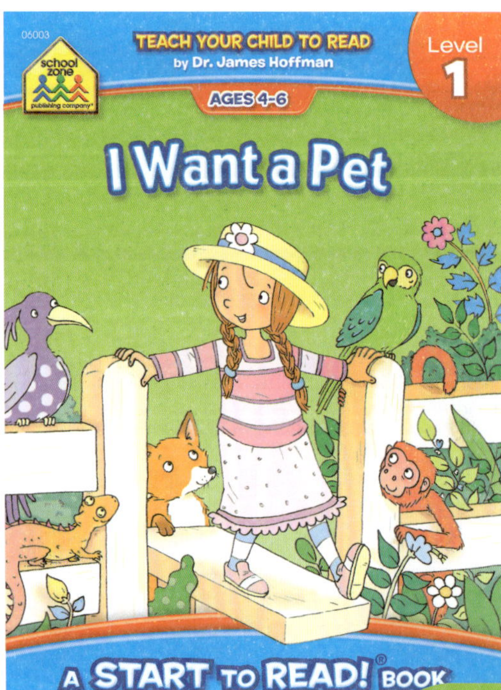

Got it! Not yet

You need: BIG TRUCKS

I can point to the cover, title, and back cover on a book.

BIG TRUCKS Look at each cover.
Find and place the title sticker that matches each cover.

Got it! Not yet

I can point to the cover, title, and back cover on a book.

Circle the books showing the front covers.
Cross out the books showing the back covers.

You need:

Parent Tip:
Every time you read a book, ask your child to find the front cover of the book and the back cover of the book.

Got it! Not yet

You need:

Let's have some fun!

Draw a line from the to the.

Got it! Not yet

You need:

I can understand the job of an author and illustrator.

An **author** is the person who writes the words in a book.

An **illustrator** is the person who creates the pictures in a book.

Online Extra:
To go to this activity, use your smartphone camera, hover over this code, and click on the link. Or go to: **anywhereteacher.com/qr/14161/02.**

Draw a line from **author** and **illustrator** to what each person did in the book.

Author | **Illustrator**

Got it! Not yet

You need:

I can understand the job of an author and illustrator.

Circle the book cover that matches the title.

A New Bike

Jog, Frog, Jog

Nicole Digs a Hole

Got it! Not yet

You need:

I can understand the job of an author and illustrator.

Draw a line from each title to the picture that matches it.

 **Hug Bug**

 **The Big Game**

 **Raccoon on the Moon**

 **It's Magic**

Parent Tip:
Find the <u>Charlie Digs</u> book. Point to the parts of the book the author did. Point to the parts that the illustrator did.

Got it! Not yet

You need:

I can identify colors.

Color the pictures in each row that should be orange.

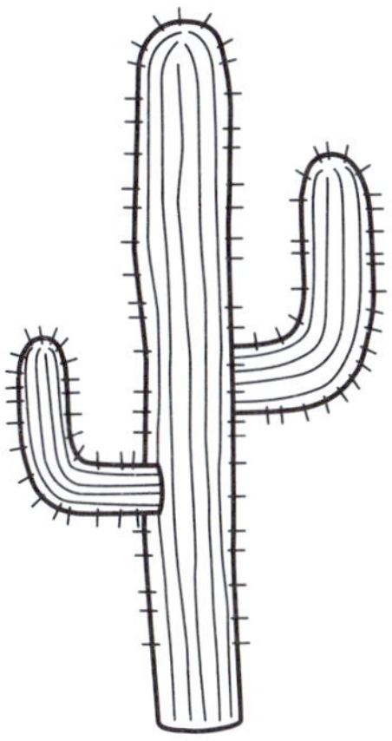

Color the pictures in each row that should be blue.

Color the pictures in each row that should be brown.

Got it! Not yet

I can identify colors.

Color the  red.

Color the  yellow.

Color the  purple.

Color the  green.

Color the  orange.

Color the  blue.

Color the  brown.

Color the  pink.

Color the  black.

Color the  gray.

Leave the  white.

You need:

Got it!   Not yet

I can tear paper.

You need:

Pinch the paper firmly between your thumb and first finger on both sides of the paper where you want to tear. Pull the paper in opposite directions.

Tear the paper on the next page into pieces.

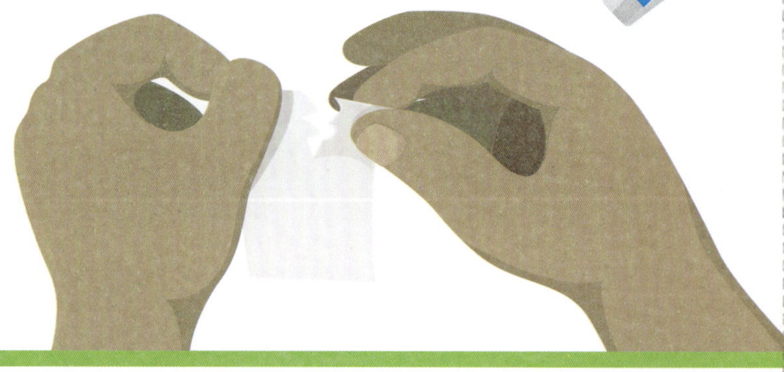

Paste the torn paper pieces onto the scene below to color the shapes.

Got it! Not yet

I can get help from my parents to read this page.

Fine Motor Skills

It's important to strengthen the muscles in your child's hands to develop good fine motor skills. Having well developed fine motor skills are the foundation of success in preschool, whether it is turning pages in a book, cutting out shapes, or writing with a pencil. Here are some activities to try.

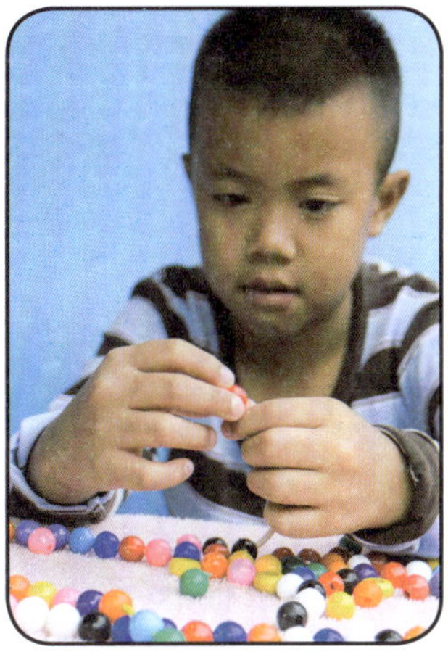

Handwriting

Why is handwriting important? It is important that your child properly forms their letters. Proper letter formation will allow your child to be an efficient writer.

When practicing your handwriting:

- **Proper grip is important when writing, tracing, and coloring.**
- **All letters are formed starting at the top.**
- **Use many different utensils to practice (e.g. markers, crayons, scissors, pens, etc.).**
- **Letters sit on the line.**
  Example: got

Most lowercase letters should be formed using one stroke (minus dotting **i**, **j**, and crossing **f**, **t**, and the letters **x** and **k**).

I can write the letters of the alphabet.

You need:

Trace the letters with your finger.

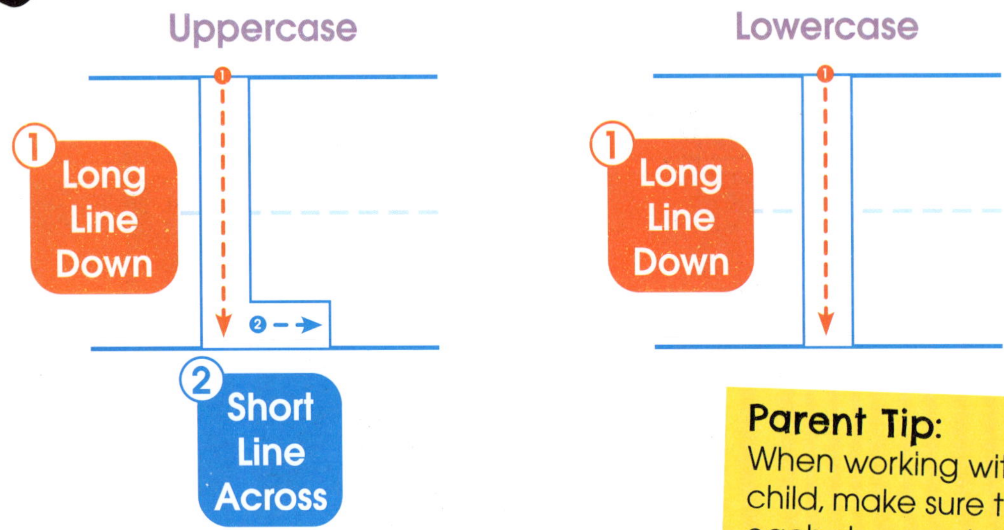

Parent Tip: When working with your child, make sure they follow each step each time.

Trace and write the letters.
Start at the red dot (●).

Practice writing the letter.

Got it! Not yet

I can identify letters and letter sounds.

You need:

Circle the pictures that start with **L**.

Use three different color crayons to color the letter.

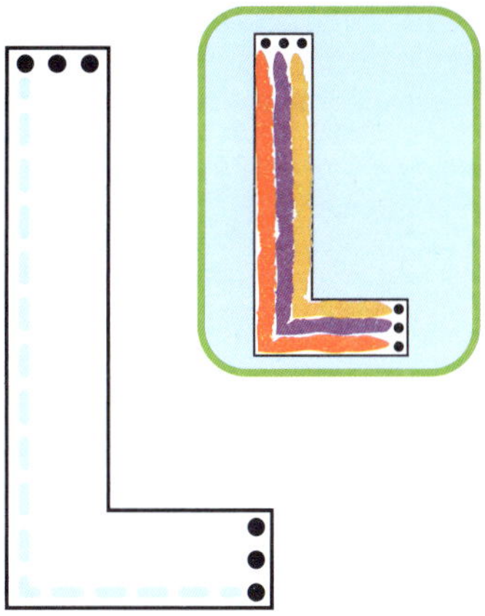

Trace the path.

Online Extra:
To go to this activity, use your smartphone camera, hover over this code, and click on the link. Or go to: **anywhereteacher.com/qr/14161/03.**

Circle all the **L**'s.

L T L F L

L L I L E L

Got it! Not yet

I can write the letters of the alphabet.

You need:

Trace the letters with your finger.

Uppercase

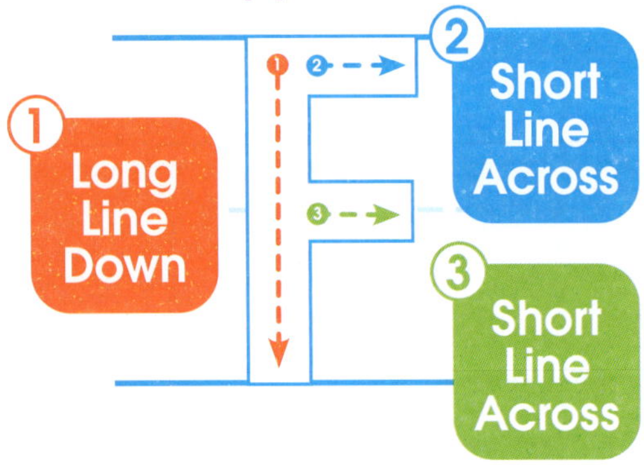

Lowercase

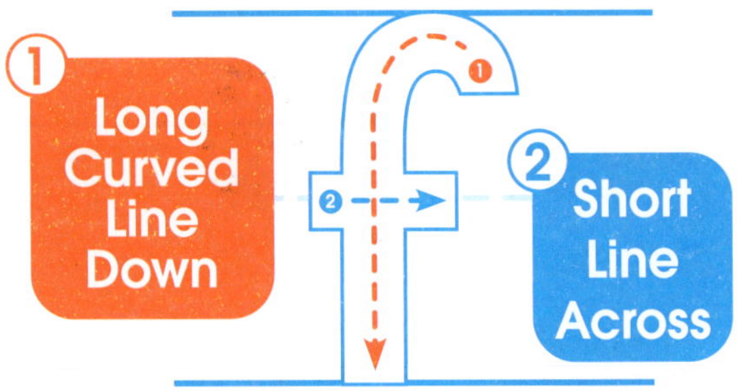

Trace and write the letters.
Start at the red dot (●).

Practice writing the letter.

Got it! Not yet

I can identify letters and letter sounds.

You need:

Some words that start with **F** are:

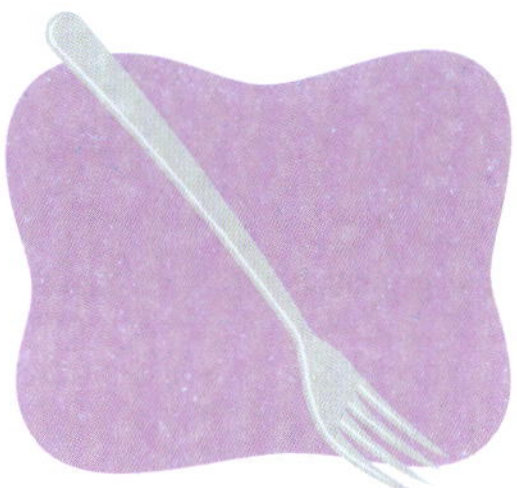

fork

fan

feather

fire

flag

Color the **Ff**'s **red**.

T F f t F f E i L F F f I f T f H

Online Extra: To go to this activity, use your smartphone camera, hover over this code, and click on the link. Or go to: **anywhereteacher.com/qr/14161/04**.

Circle the pictures that start with **F**.

Got it! Not yet

You need:

I can write the letters of the alphabet.

Trace the letters with your finger.

Uppercase

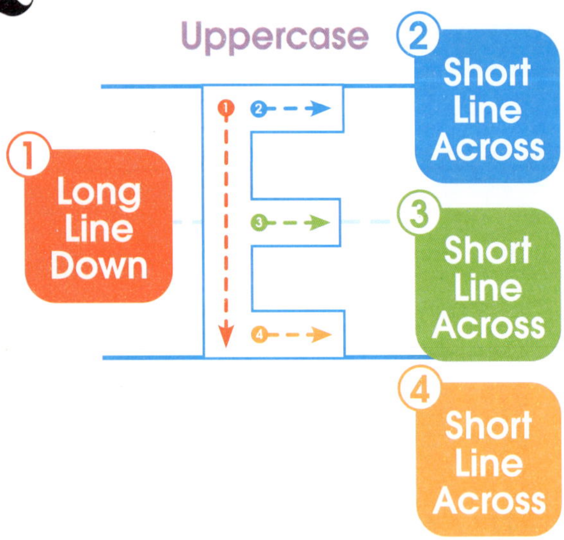

Lowercase

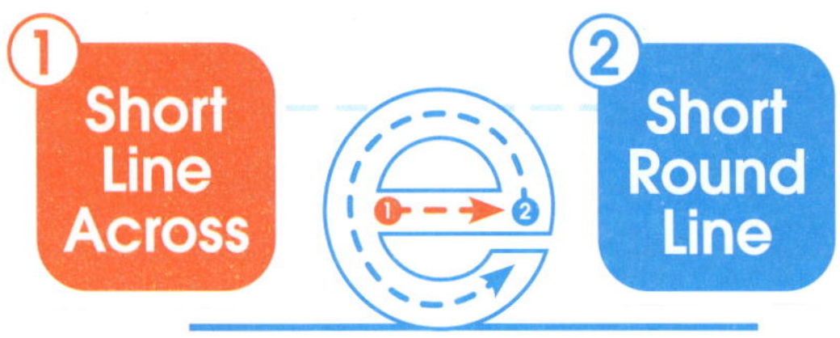

Online Extra:
To go to this activity, use your smartphone camera, hover over this code, and click on the link. Or go to: **anywhereteacher.com/qr/14161/18.**

Trace and write the letters.
Start at the red dot (●).

Practice writing the letter.

Got it! Not yet

I can identify letters and letter sounds.

You need:

Cut along the dotted lines.
Fold each page on the blue line.
Put the pages in order together to make your own **Ee** book.

E

fold

My Letter

E

Book

E is for **elephant**!

fold

E is for **egg**!

E is for **elk**!

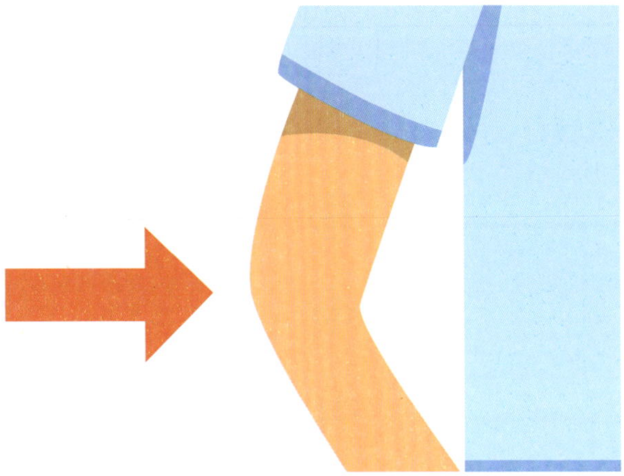

E is for **elbow**!

E is for **envelope**!

E is for **elf**!

I can identify letters and letter sounds.

You need:

Cut out the letter squares.
Glue them into the correct squares.

Uppercase E

Lowercase e

E	e
e	E
E	e
e	E
E	e
E	e
e	E

Got it! Not yet

I can identify letters and letter sounds.

You need:

Circle the letter that begins each picture word.

L F E

L F E

L F E

L F E

L F E

L F E

Color the **Ll**'s blue.
Color the **Ff**'s green.
Color the **Ee**'s orange.

E F L E F e e f L f l l E L e F f l

Got it! Not yet

I can identify letters and letter sounds.

You need:

The letter **Hh** makes the sound you hear in words like:

hat

heart

hot dog

Circle the things in the picture that start with **Hh**.

Got it! Not yet

I can write the letters of the alphabet.

You need:

Trace the letters with your finger.

Uppercase

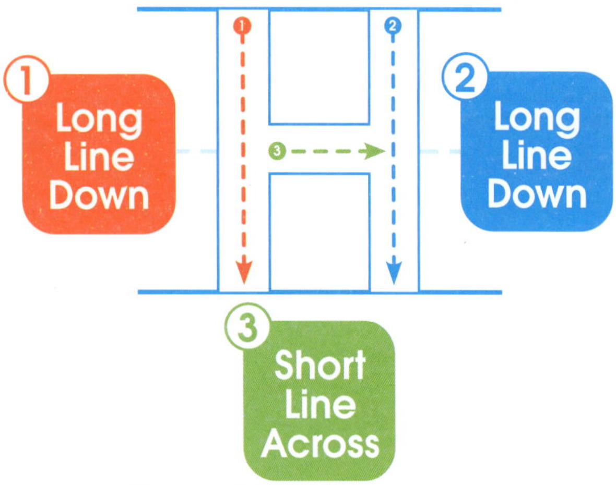

Lowercase

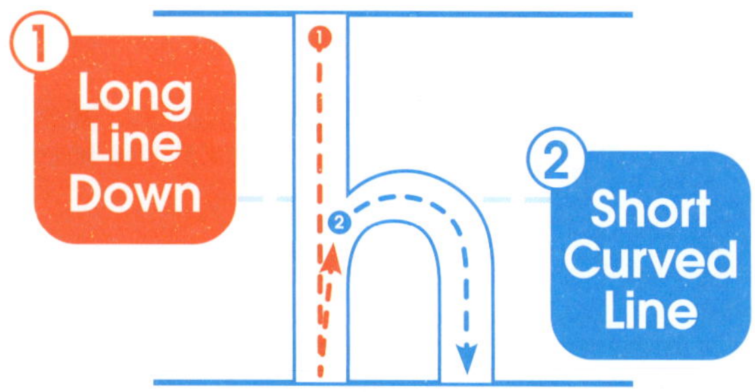

Parent Tip:
You do not pick up your pencil when writing lowercase **h**.

Trace and write the letters.
Start at the red dot (●).

Practice writing the letter.

Got it! Not yet

I can identify letters and letter sounds.

You need: scissors, GLUE

Cut out the letter squares.
Glue them into the correct squares.

I am an H

I am NOT an H

H	T
H	H
I	F
H	H
L	K
H	X
E	H
H	Y
H	A

Got it! Not yet

Let's have some fun!

Draw a line from the  to her home .

You need:

Finish

Got it! Not yet

I can write the letters of the alphabet.

You need:

Trace the letters with your finger.

Uppercase

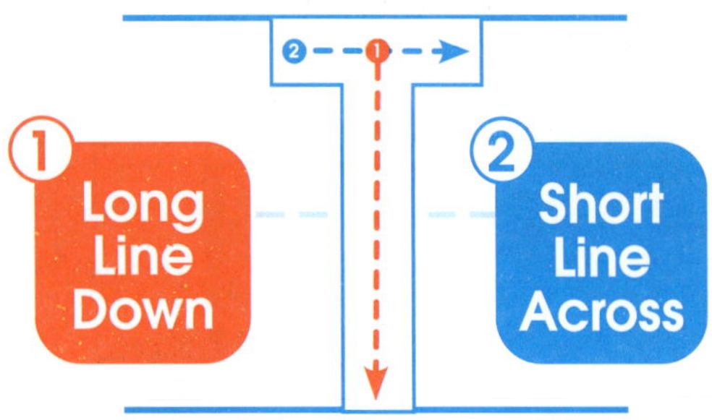

Lowercase

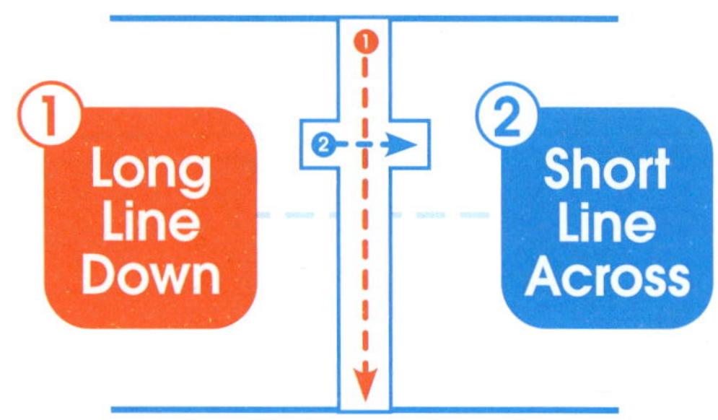

Trace and write the letters.
Start at the red dot (●).

Practice writing the letter.

Got it! Not yet

I can identify letters and letter sounds.

You need:

Color the pictures that start with **T**.

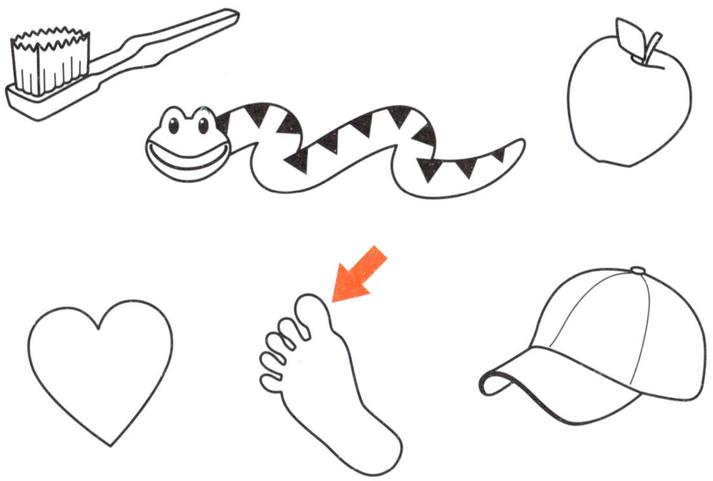

Use three different color crayons to color the letter.

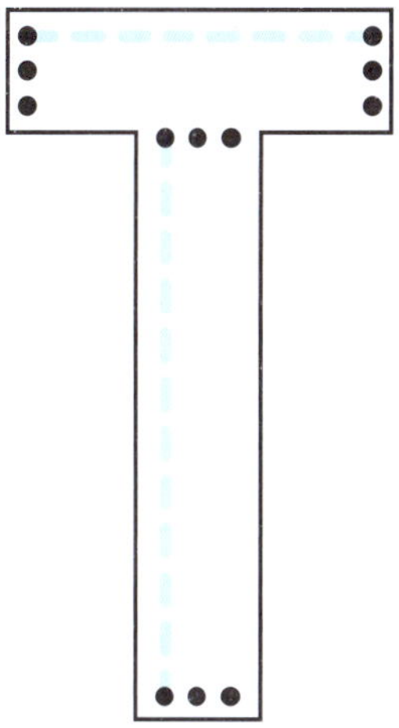

Trace the path.

Circle all the **T**'s.

Got it! Not yet

I can write the letters of the alphabet.

Trace the letters with your finger.

Uppercase

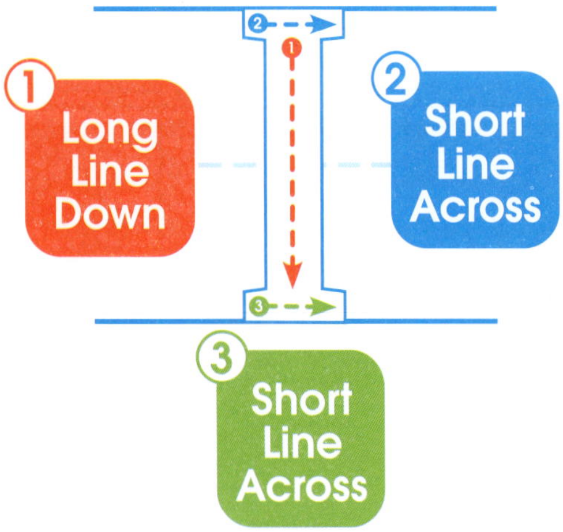

Lowercase

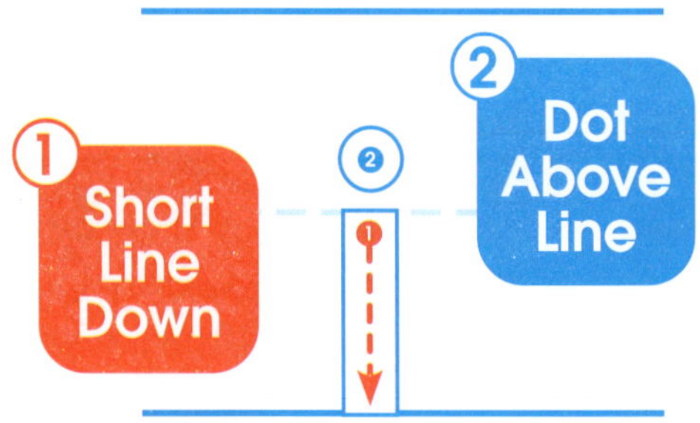

Trace and write the letters.
Start at the red dot (●).

Practice writing the letter.

Got it! Not yet

I can identify letters and letter sounds.

You need:

Cut along the dotted lines.
Fold each page on the blue line.
Put the pages in order together to make your own **Ii** book.

I

fold

My Letter

I

Book

I is for
iguana!

fold

I is for
igloo!

I is for **inchworm**!

I is for **insect**!

I is for **ink**!

I is for **ill**!

I can identify letters and letter sounds.

You need:

Match the uppercase letters with the lowercase letters. Use a different color crayon for each letter.

L F E T I H

e h f l i t

Got it! Not yet

I can write the letters of the alphabet.

You need:

Trace the letters with your finger.

Uppercase

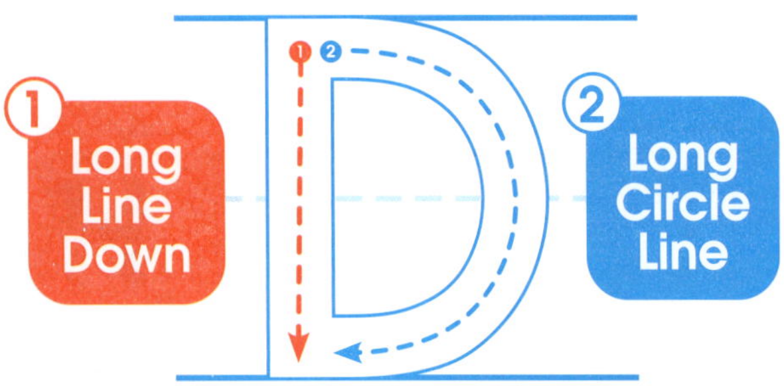

Lowercase

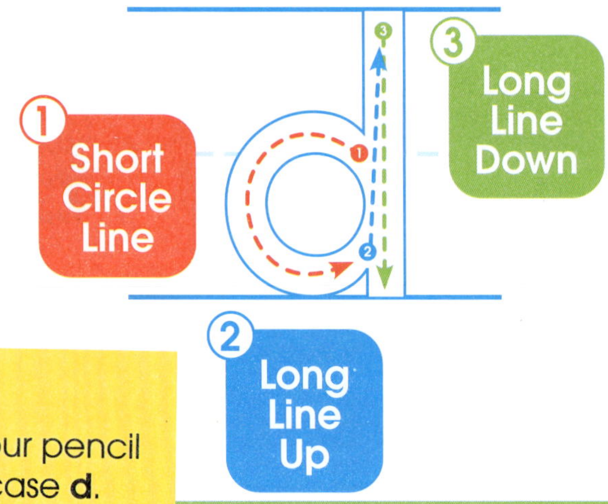

Parent Tip:
You do not pick up your pencil when writing a lowercase **d**.

Trace and write the letters.
Start at the red dot (•).

Practice writing the letter.

Got it! Not yet

I can identify letters and letter sounds.

You need:

The letter **Dd** makes the sound you hear in words like:

doll

deer

door

dog

donkey

Circle the things in the picture that start with **Dd**.

Got it! Not yet

I can write the letters of the alphabet.

You need:

Trace the letters with your finger.

Uppercase

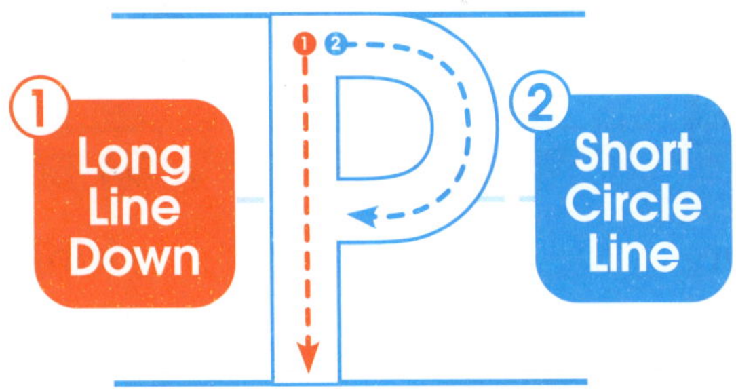

Lowercase

Parent Tip:
You do not pick up your pencil when writing lowercase **p**.

Trace and write the letters.
Start at the red dot (●).

P P P

p p p

Practice writing the letter.

Got it! Not yet

I can identify letters and letter sounds.

You need:

Some words that start with **P** are:

paper

pear

pig

pie

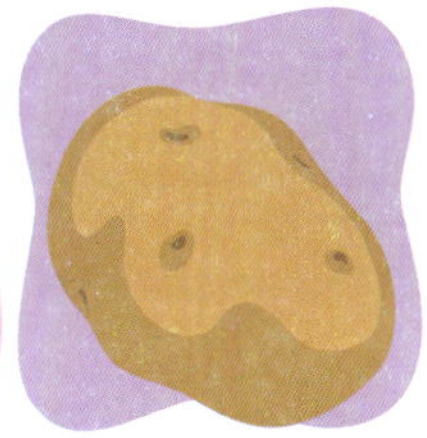
potato

popcorn

Color the **Pp**'s purple.

P p B c p P p P P P p d P p D q D b p

Online Extra: To go to this activity, use your smartphone camera, hover over this code, and click on the link. Or go to: **anywhereteacher.com/qr/14161/05.**

Circle the pictures that start with **P**.

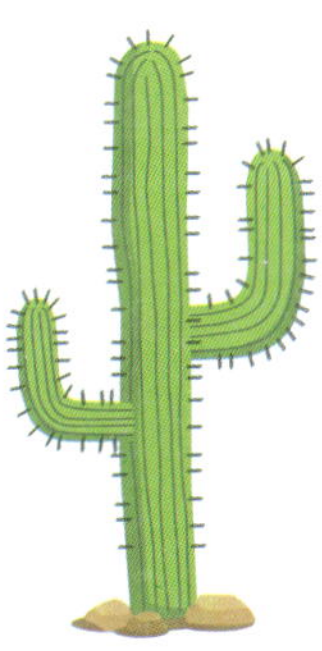

Got it! Not yet

I can write the letters of the alphabet.

Trace the letters with your finger.

Uppercase

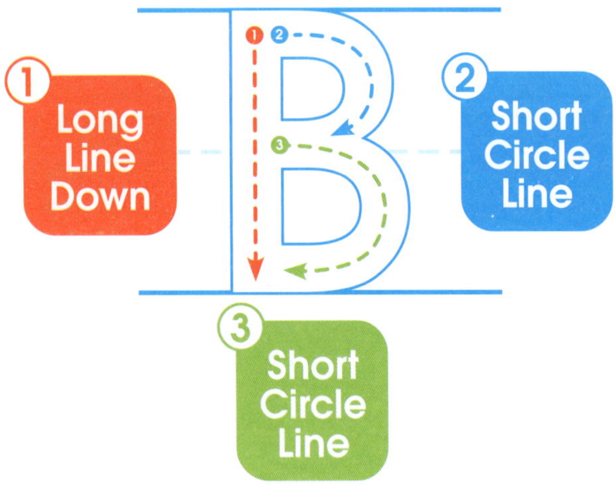

Lowercase

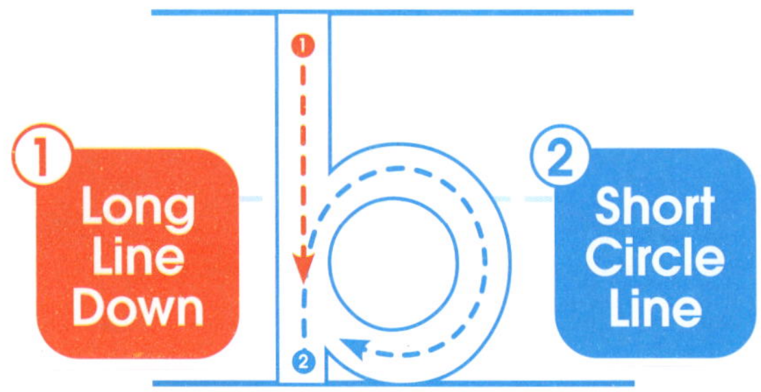

Parent Tip:
You do not pick up your pencil when writing lowercase **b**.

Trace and write the letters.
Start at the red dot (•).

B B B

b b b

Practice writing the letter.

Got it! Not yet

I can identify letters and letter sounds.

You need:

Some words that start with **B** are:

bird

ball

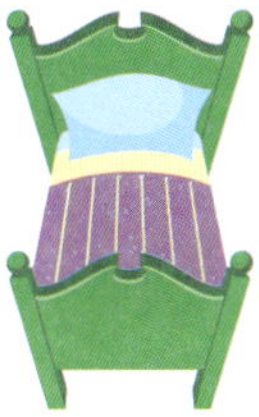
bed

basket

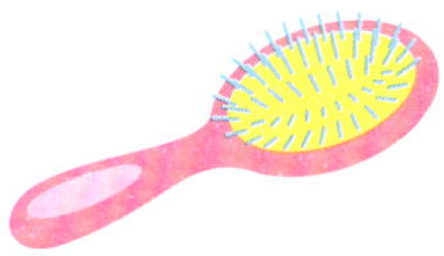
brush

button

Use three different color crayons to color the letter.

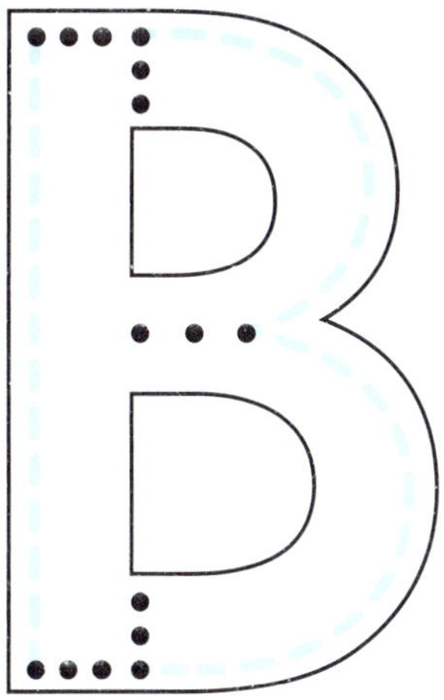

Trace the path.

Circle all the pictures that start with **B**.

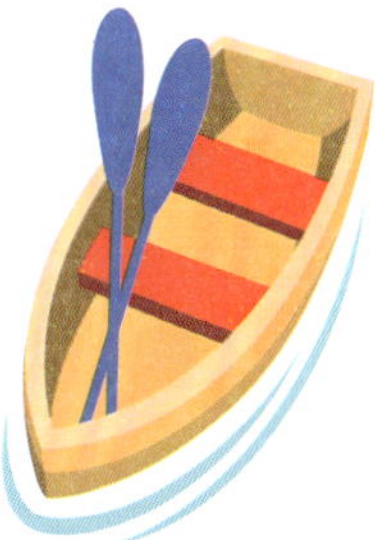

Got it! Not yet

I can write the letters of the alphabet.

You need:

Trace the letters with your finger.

Uppercase

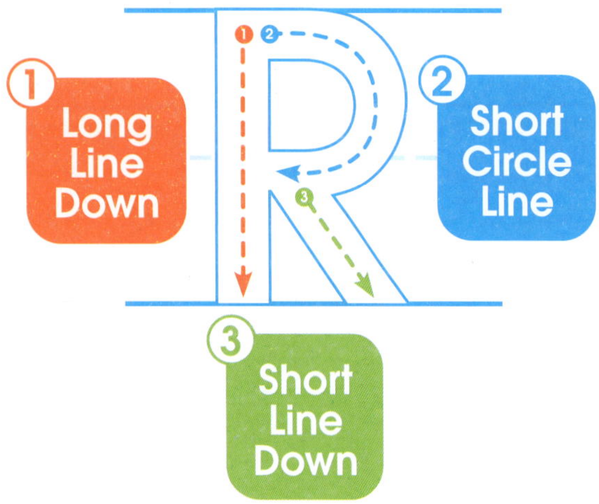

Lowercase

Parent Tip:
You do not pick up your pencil when writing lowercase **r**.

Trace and write the letters.
Start at the red dot (●).

Practice writing the letter.

Got it! Not yet

I can identify letters and letter sounds.

You need:

The letter **Rr** makes the sound you hear in words like:

ring

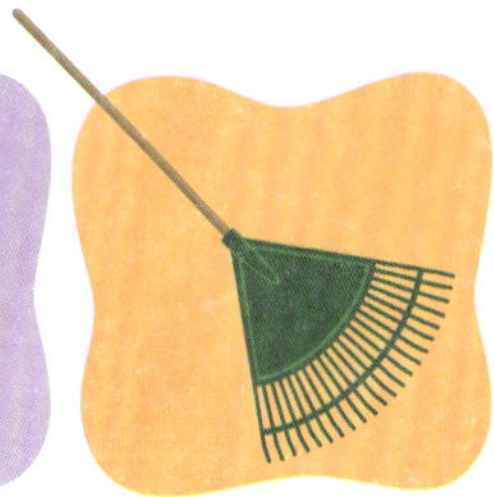
rake

rhinoceros

rock

rat

rose

Circle the things in the picture that start with **Rr**.

Got it! Not yet

I can write the letters of the alphabet.

You need:

Trace the letters with your finger.

Uppercase	Lowercase
1 Long Circle Line	1 Short Circle Line

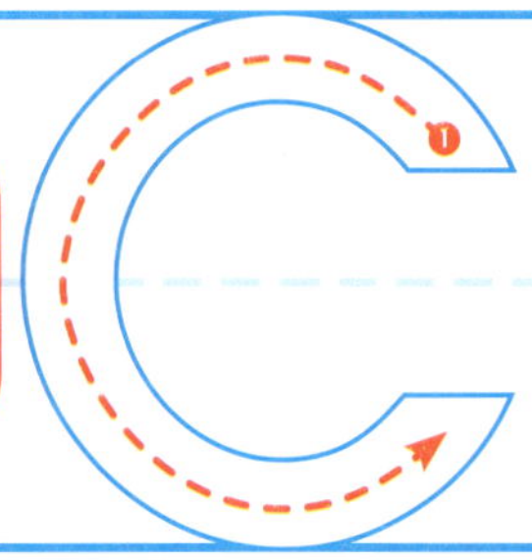

Trace and write the letters.
Start at the red dot (●).

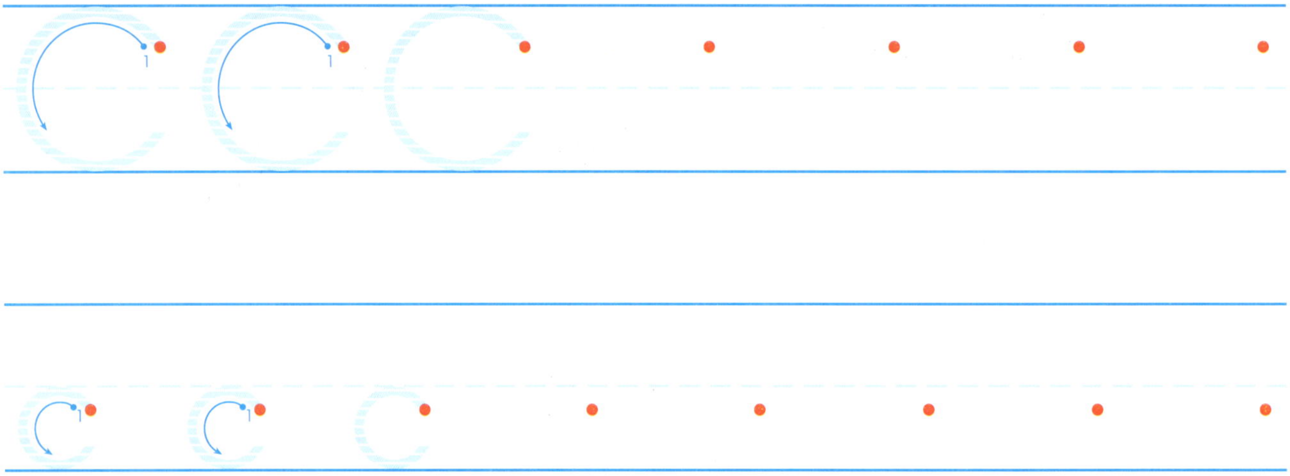

Practice writing the letter.

Got it! Not yet

You need:

I can identify letters and letter sounds.

Some words that start with **C** are:

carrot

camel

can

clock

corn

cow

Color the **Cc**'s red.

C Q C p a

G b O C C c

c a c G c O

Use a crayon to **underline** the words that start with the **C** sound.

Online Extra:
To go to this activity, use your smartphone camera, hover over this code, and click on the link. Or go to: **anywhereteacher.com/qr/14161/06**.

The cat wore a crown and sat by a cactus eating cake.

Got it! Not yet

I can write the letters of the alphabet.

You need:

Trace the letters with your finger.

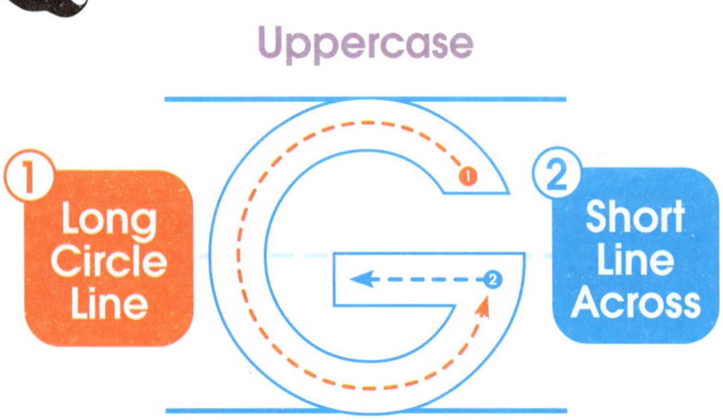

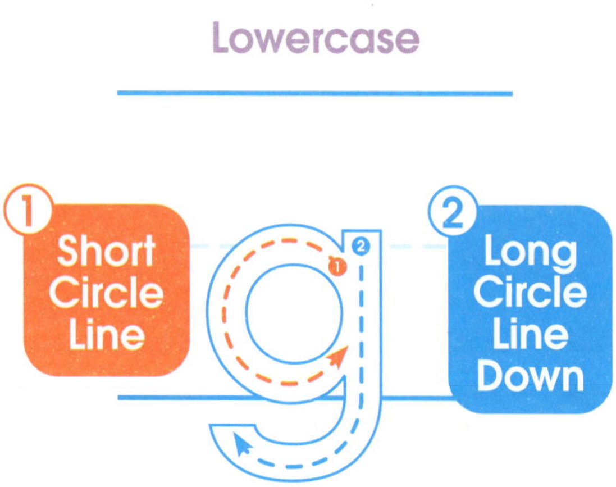

Parent Tip:
You do not pick up your pencil when writing lowercase **g**.

Trace and write the letters.
Start at the red dot (●).

Practice writing the letter.

Got it! Not yet

I can identify letters and letter sounds.

You need:

Circle all the **G**'s.

G C G O G G

G Q G G C O

Trace the path.

Color the pictures that start with **G**.

Use three different color crayons to color the letter.

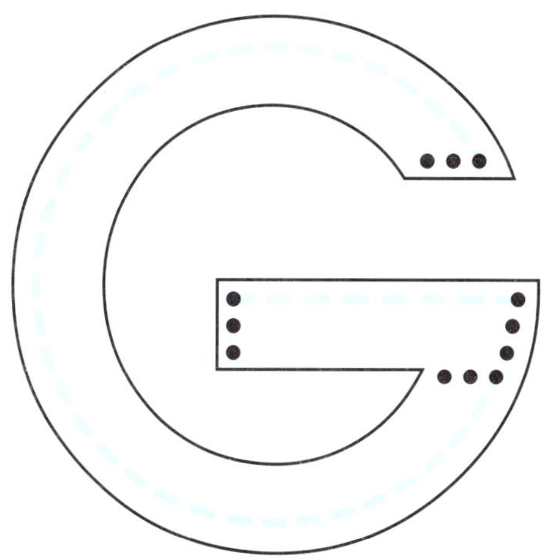

Got it! Not yet

I can write the letters of the alphabet.

You need:

Trace the letters with your finger.

Uppercase

① Long Circle Line

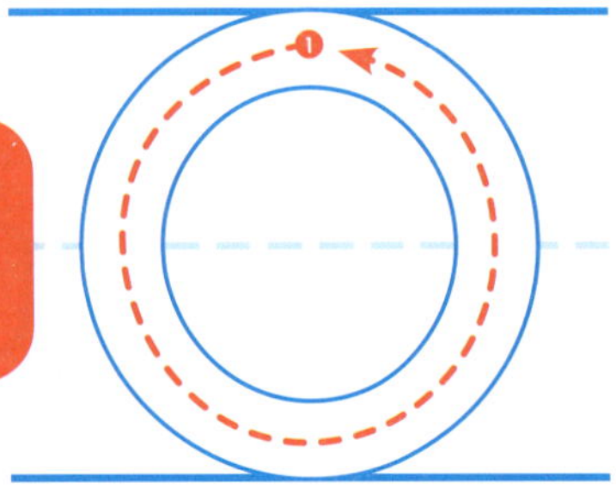

Lowercase

① Short Circle Line

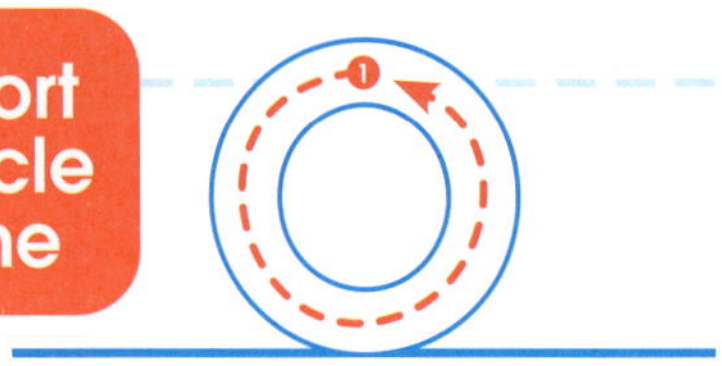

Trace and write the letters.
Start at the red dot (●).

Practice writing the letter.

Got it! Not yet

I can identify letters and letter sounds.

You need:

Cut along the dotted lines.
Fold each page on the blue line.
Put the pages in order together to make your own **Oo** book.

O

O

fold

My Letter

O

Book

O is for **otter**!

fold

O is for **octopus**!

O is for **ostrich**!

O is for **olive**!

O is for **ox**!

O is for **octagon**!

I can identify letters and letter sounds.

You need:

Say the name of each picture.
Write the letter **o** next to the pictures that begin with **o**.
Color the pictures that begin with the letter **o**.

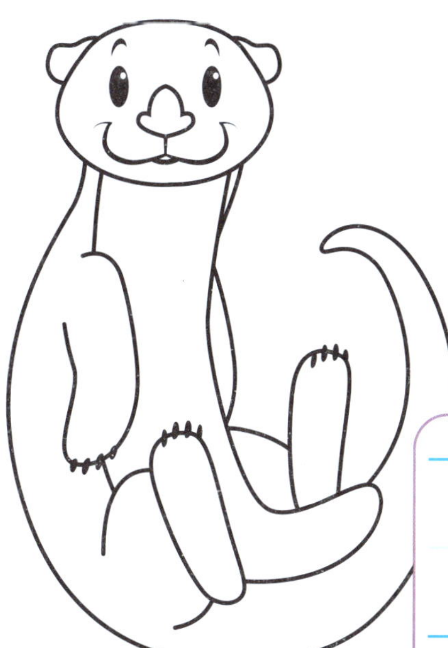

Got it! Not yet

I can write the letters of the alphabet.

You need:

Trace the letters with your finger.

Uppercase

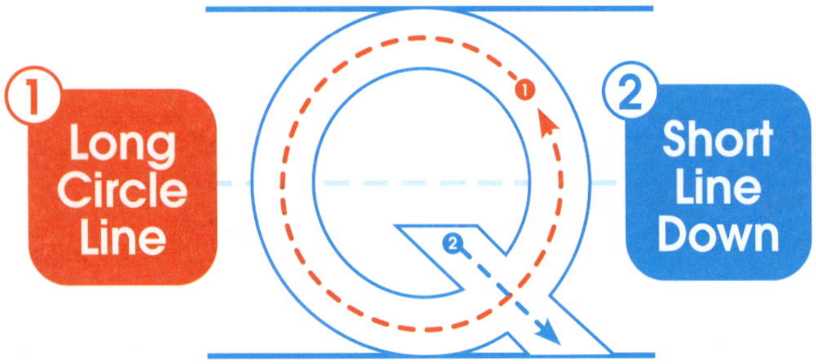

Lowercase

Parent Tip:
You do not pick up your pencil when writing lowercase **q**.

Trace and write the letters.
Start at the red dot (●).

Practice writing the letter.

Got it! Not yet

I can identify letters and letter sounds.

You need:

Say the name of each picture.
Write the letter **Q** next to the pictures that begin with **Q**.
Color the pictures that begin with the letter **Q**.

Got it! Not yet

I can write the letters of the alphabet.

You need:

Trace the letters with your finger.

Uppercase

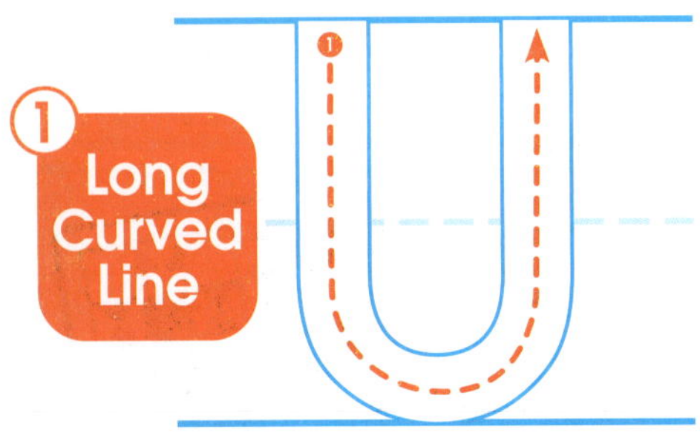

Lowercase

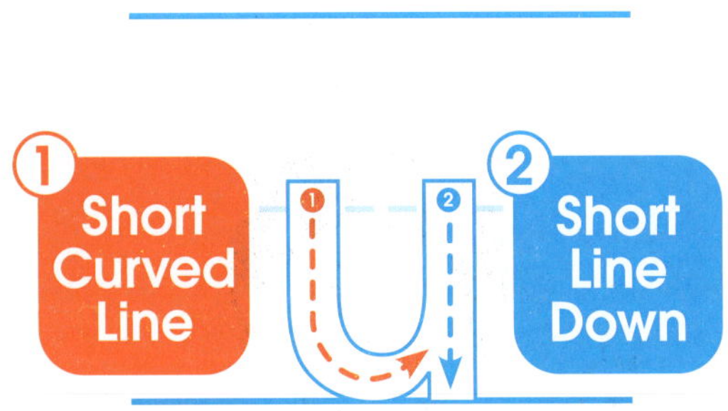

Parent Tip:
You do not pick up your pencil when writing lowercase **u**.

Trace and write the letters.
Start at the red dot (●).

Practice writing the letter.

Got it! Not yet

You need:

I can identify letters and letter sounds.

Cut along the dotted lines.
Fold each page on the blue line.
Put the pages in order together to make your own **Uu** book.

U

fold

My Letter

U

Book

U is for **umbrella**!

fold

U is for **umpire**!

U is for **underwear**!

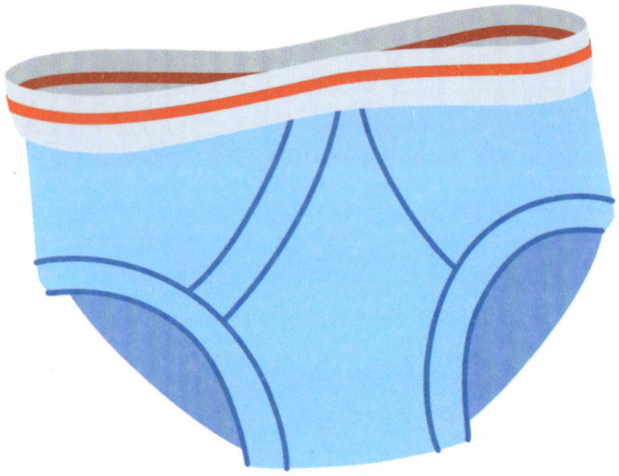

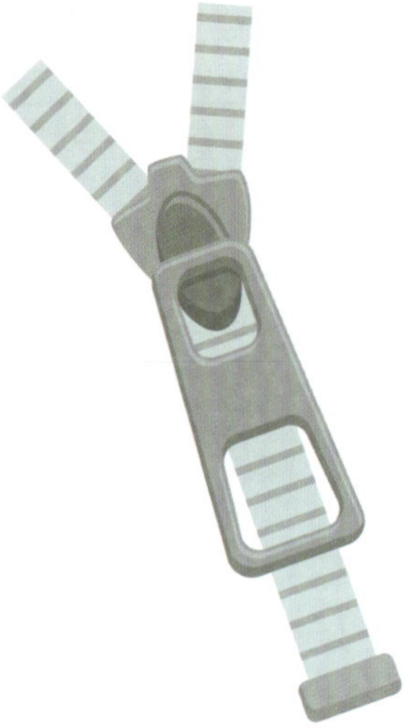

U is for **unzip**!

U is for **up**!

U is for **under**!

Got it! Not yet

I can identify letters and letter sounds.

You need:

Say the name of each picture.
Write the letter **U** next to the pictures that begin with **U**.
Color the pictures that begin with the letter **U**.

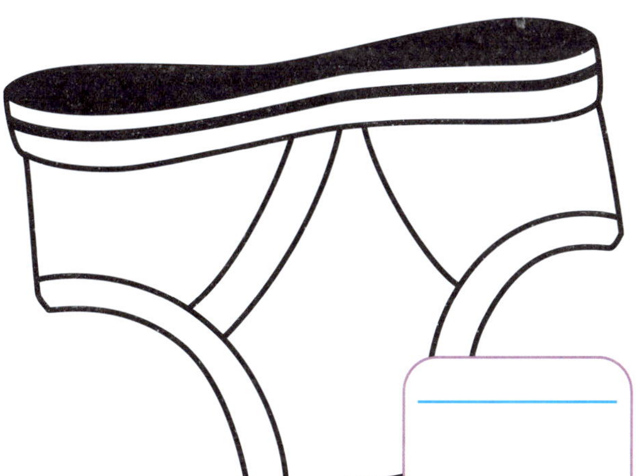

Got it! Not yet

I can write the letters of the alphabet.

You need:

Trace the letters with your finger.

Uppercase

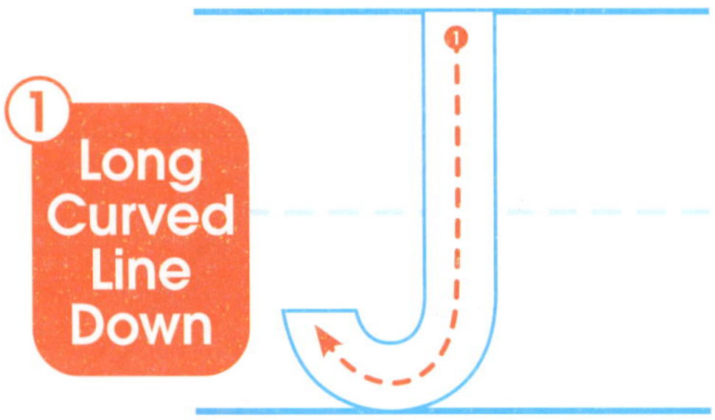

Lowercase

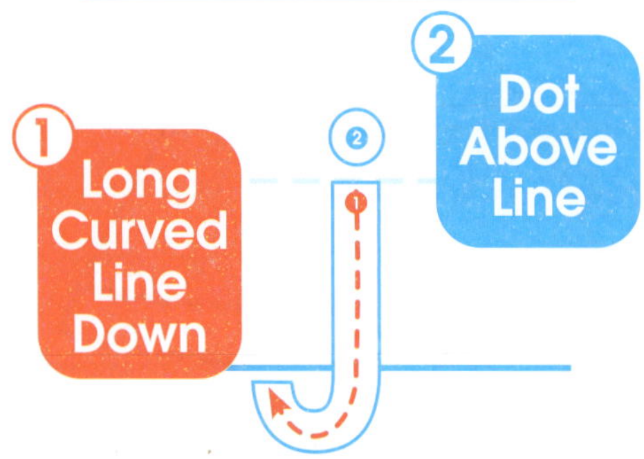

Online Extra:
To go to this activity, use your smartphone camera, hover over this code, and click on the link. Or go to: **anywhereteacher.com/qr/14161/19.**

Trace and write the letters.
Start at the red dot (●).

Practice writing the letter.

Got it! Not yet

I can identify letters and letter sounds.

You need:

Say the name of each picture.
Write the letter **J** next to the pictures that begin with **J**.
Color the pictures that begin with the letter **J**.

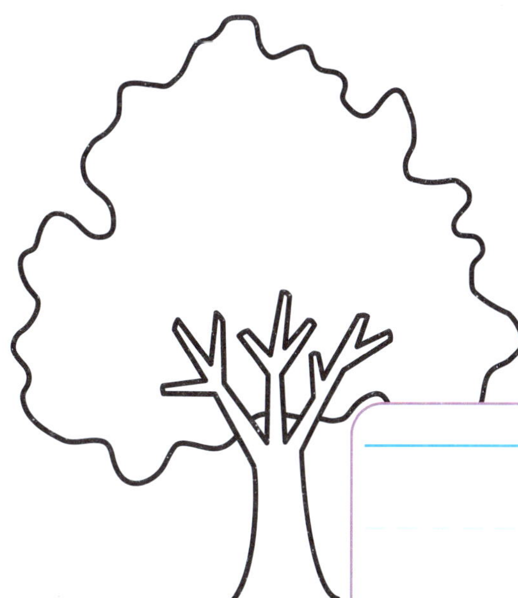

Got it! Not yet

I can write the letters of the alphabet.

You need:

Trace the letters with your finger.

Uppercase

1 Long Curved Line

S

Lowercase

1 Short Curved Line

s

Online Extra:
To go to this activity, use your smartphone camera, hover over this code, and click on the link. Or go to: **anywhereteacher.com/qr/14161/07.**

Trace and write the letters.
Start at the red dot (●).

S S S

s s s

Practice writing the letter.

Got it! Not yet

I can identify letters and letter sounds.

You need:

The letter **Ss** makes the sound you hear in words like:

snail snake snowflake sock soap sun

Help Socrates find his scissors.
Trace a path through the **Ss** letters.

Got it! Not yet

I can write the letters of the alphabet.

You need:

Trace the letters with your finger.

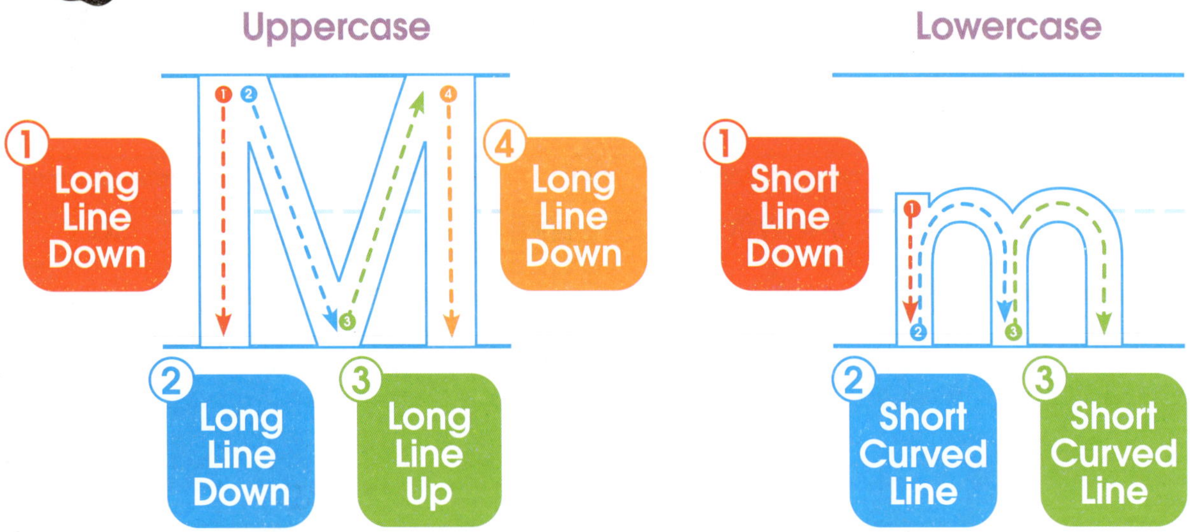

Trace and write the letters.
Start at the red dot (•).

Practice writing the letter.

Got it! Not yet

I can identify letters and letter sounds.

You need:

The letter **Mm** makes the sound you hear in words like:

map

mushroom

mitten

mop

monkey

milk

Circle the things in the picture that start with **Mm**.

Got it! Not yet

I can write the letters of the alphabet.

You need:

Trace the letters with your finger.

Uppercase | Lowercase

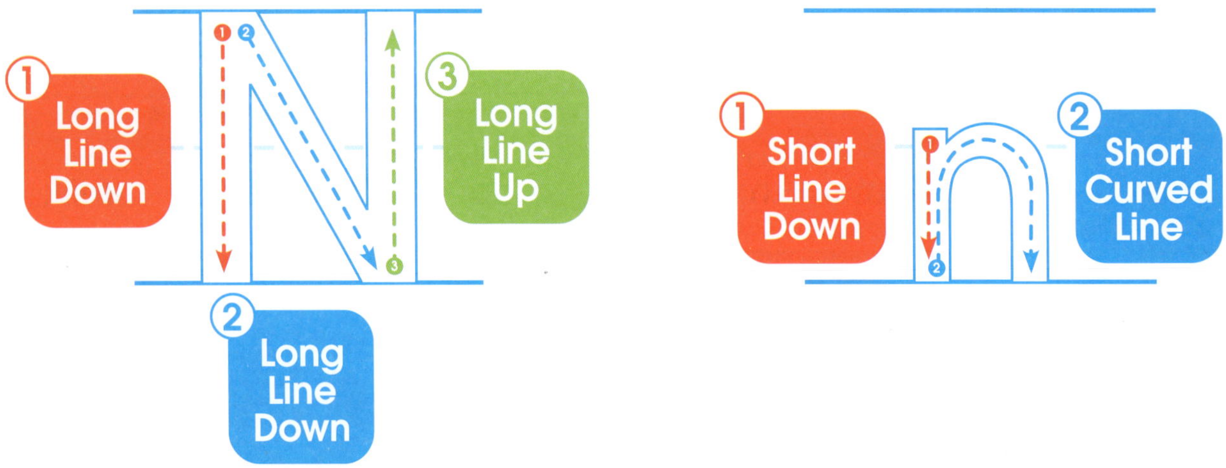

Trace and write the letters.
Start at the red dot (•).

Practice writing the letter.

Got it! Not yet

I can identify letters and letter sounds.

You need:

The letter **Nn** makes the sound you hear in words like:

nail

nuts

net

nest

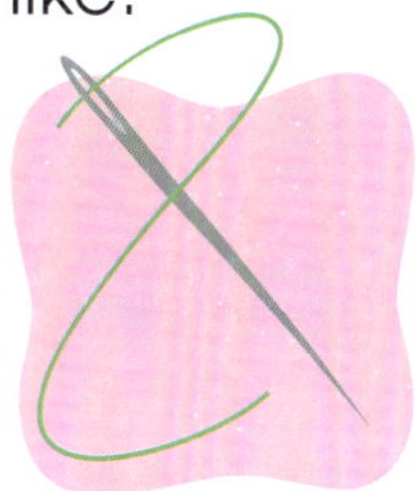
needle

nachos

Help Nestor find his notebook.
Trace a path through the **Nn** letters.

Got it! Not yet

I can write the letters of the alphabet.

You need:

Trace the letters with your finger.

Uppercase

1 Long Line Down

2 Long Line Down

3 Short Line Across

Lowercase

1 Short Circle Line

2 Short Line Down

Parent Tip:
You do not pick up your pencil when writing a lowercase **a**.

Trace and write the letters.
Start at the red dot (●).

Practice writing the letter.

Got it! Not yet

I can identify letters and letter sounds.

You need:

Cut along the dotted lines.
Fold each page on the blue line.
Put the pages in order together to make your own **Aa** book.

A

My Letter

A

Book

A is for **ant**!

A is for **apple**!

A is for **alligator**!

A is for **astronaut**!

A is for **arm**!

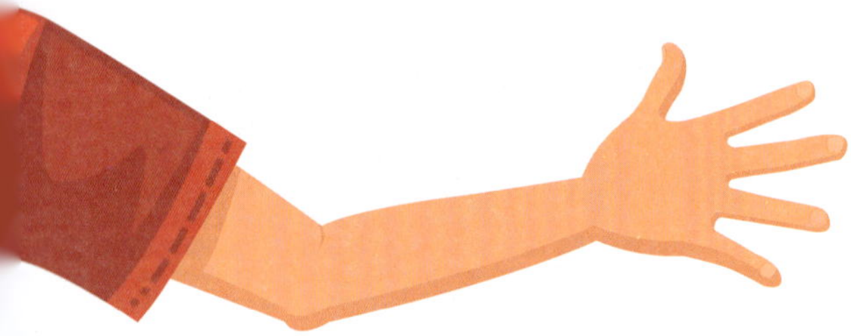

A is for **ax**!

I can identify letters and letter sounds.

You need:

Say the name of each picture.
Write the letter **A** next to the pictures that begin with **A**.
Color the pictures that begin with the letter **A**.

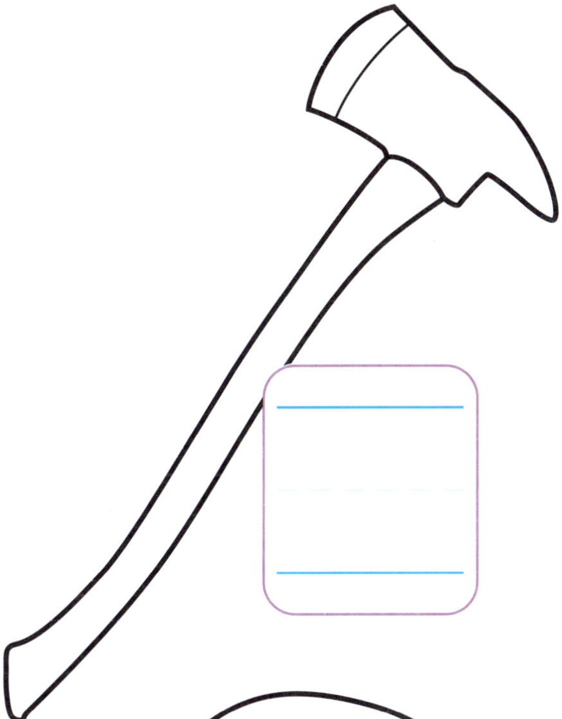

I can write the letters of the alphabet.

You need:

Trace the letters with your finger.

Uppercase

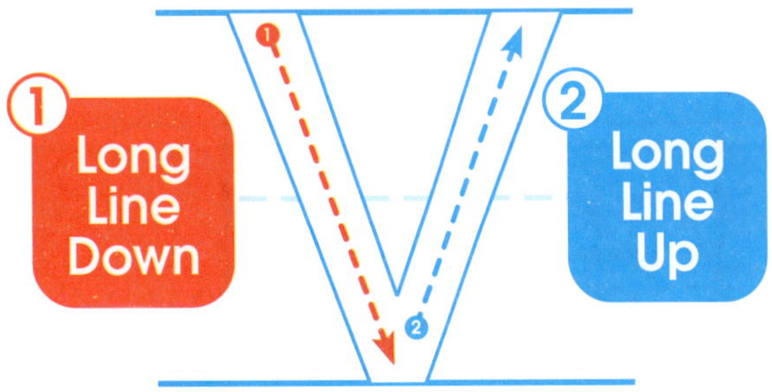

Lowercase

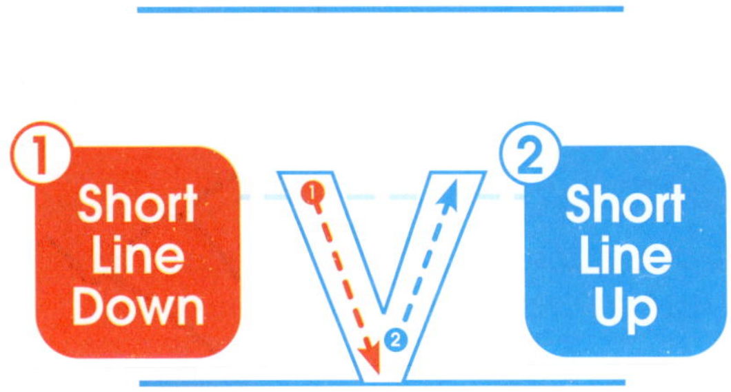

Trace and write the letters.
Start at the red dot (●).

V V V

v v v

Practice writing the letter.

Got it!   Not yet

I can identify letters and letter sounds.

You need:

Some words that start with **V** are:

vase

volcano

volleyball

vest

violin

Color the **Vv**'s purple.

V h L V y V A V V
k V v K W v W X
v Y V v V K Y A

Online Extra:
To go to this activity, use your smartphone camera, hover over this code, and click on the link. Or go to: **anywhereteacher.com/qr/14161/08**.

Trace the path.

Got it! Not yet

I can write the letters of the alphabet.

You need:

Trace the letters with your finger.

Uppercase

1 Long Line Down
2 Long Line Up
3 Long Line Down
4 Long Line Up

Lowercase

1 Short Line Down
2 Short Line Up
3 Short Line Down
4 Short Line Up

Trace and write the letters.
Start at the red dot (●).

Practice writing the letter.

Parent Tip:
You do not pick up your pencil when writing an uppercase **W** or lowercase **w**.

Got it! Not yet

I can identify letters and letter sounds.

You need:

The letter **Ww** makes the sound you hear in words like:

wagon	watch	window	watermelon	worm	wig

Circle the things in the picture that start with **Ww**.

Got it! Not yet

I can write the letters of the alphabet.

You need:

Trace the letters with your finger.

Uppercase

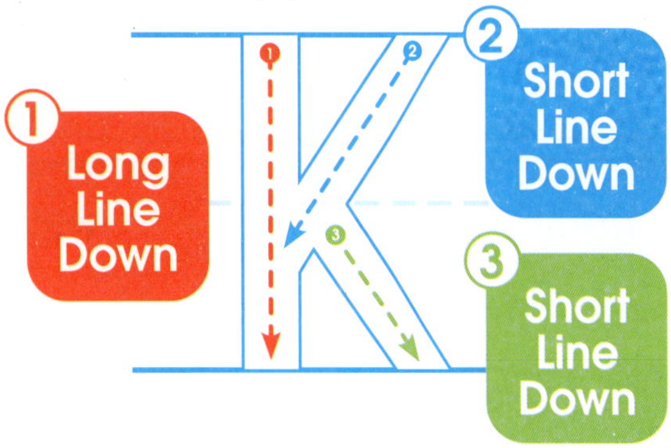

Lowercase

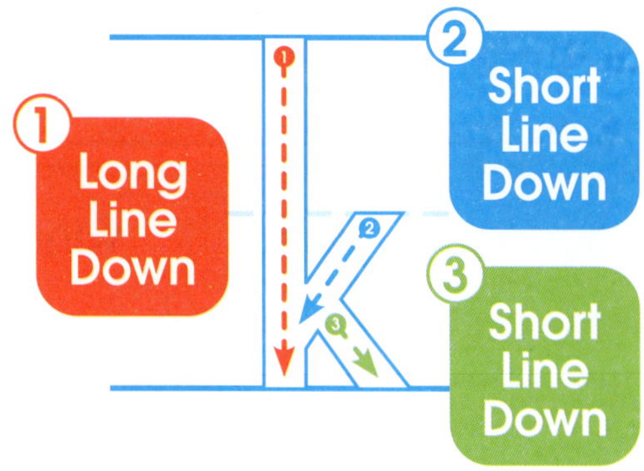

Trace and write the letters.
Start at the red dot (●).

Practice writing the letter.

Got it! Not yet

I can identify letters and letter sounds.

You need:

Some words that start with **K** are:

kettle **key** **kitten** **kite** **king** **kayak**

Color the **Kk**'s blue.

Online Extra:
To go to this activity, use your smartphone camera, hover over this code, and click on the link. Or go to:
anywhereteacher.com/qr/14161/09.

Circle the pictures that start with **K**.

Got it! Not yet

I can write the letters of the alphabet.

You need:

Trace the letters with your finger.

Uppercase

Lowercase

Trace and write the letters.
Start at the red dot (●).

Practice writing the letter.

Got it!   Not yet

I can identify letters and letter sounds.

You need:

Say the name of each picture.
Write the letter **X** next to the pictures that begin with **X**.
Color the pictures that begin with the letter **X**.

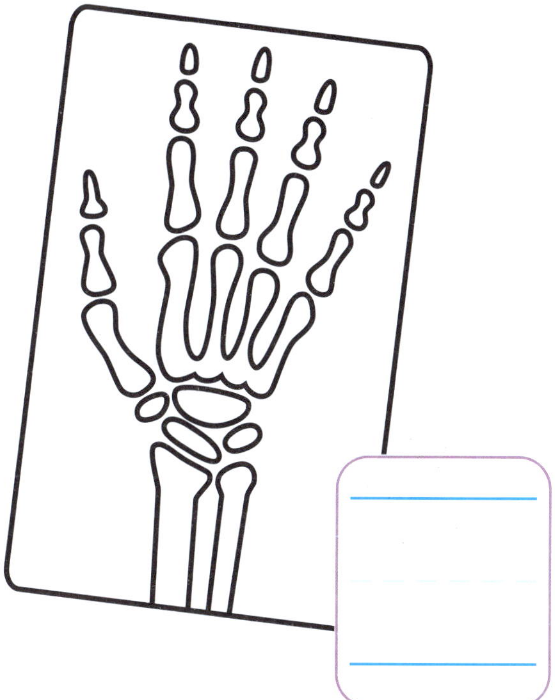

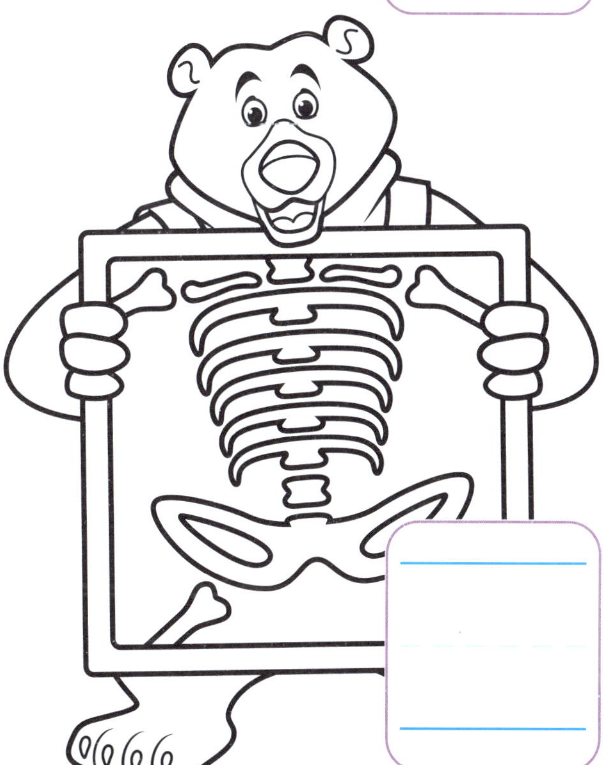

Got it! Not yet

I can write the letters of the alphabet.

You need:

Trace the letters with your finger.

Uppercase

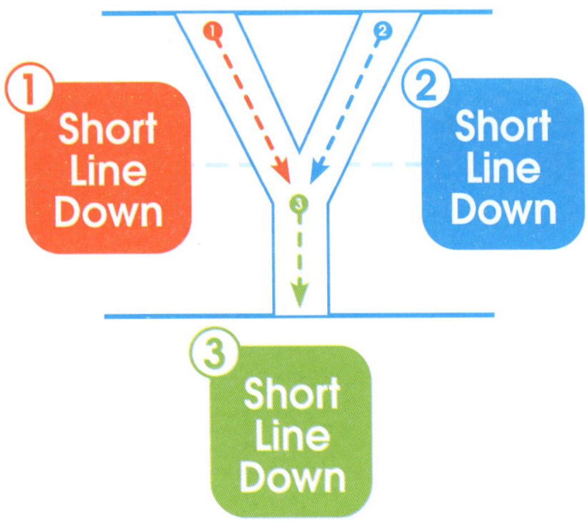

Lowercase

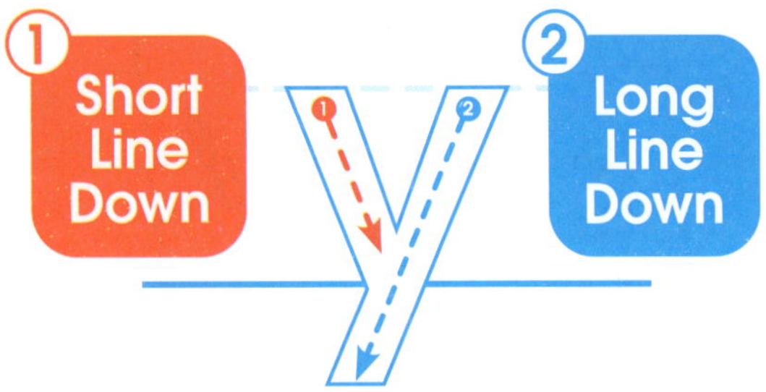

Online Extra:
To go to this activity, use your smartphone camera, hover over this code, and click on the link. Or go to: **anywhereteacher.com/qr/14161/10.**

Trace and write the letters.
Start at the red dot (●).

Practice writing the letter.

Got it! Not yet

I can identify letters and letter sounds.

You need:

Color the pictures that start with **Y**.

Use three different color crayons to color the letter.

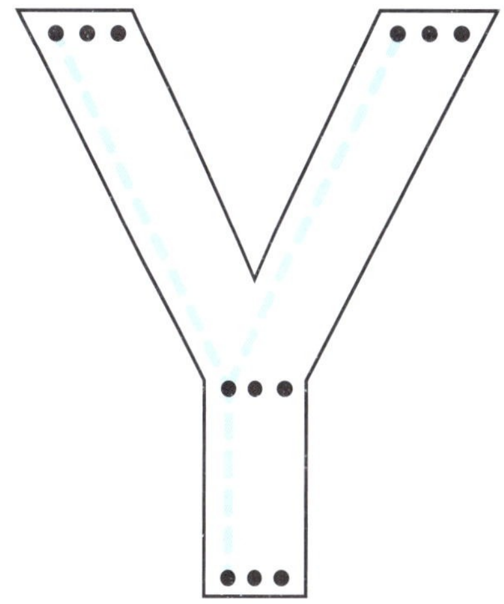

Trace the path.

Circle all the **Y**'s.

Y K Y L Y Y

Y X Y Y K X

Got it! Not yet

I can write the letters of the alphabet.

You need:

Trace the letters with your finger.

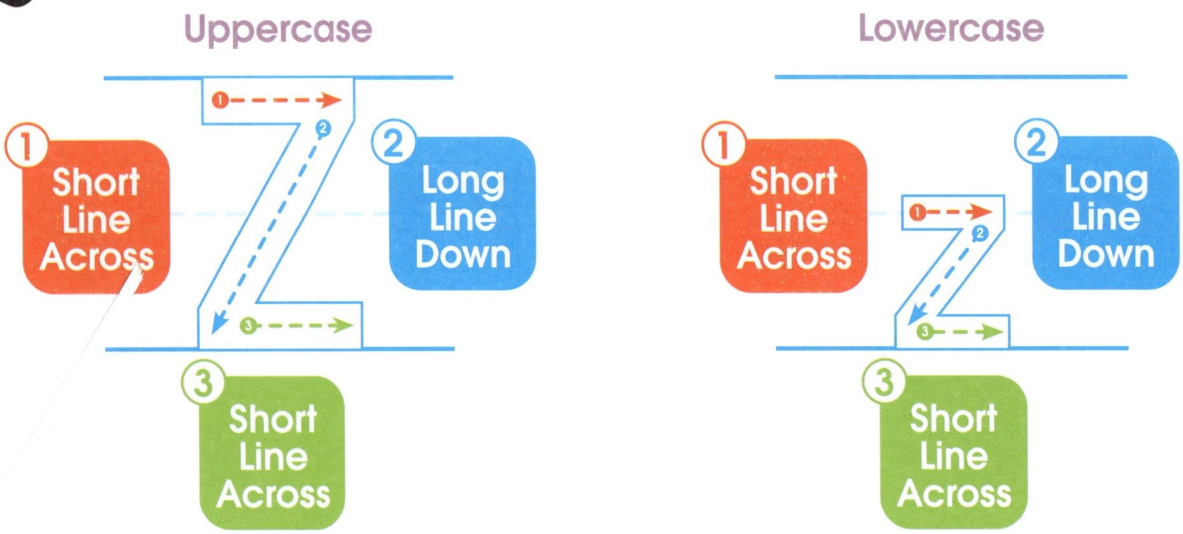

Trace and write the letters.
Start at the red dot (●).

Practice writing the letter.

Parent Tip:
You do not pick up your pencil when writing an uppercase **Z** and lowercase **z**.

Got it! Not yet

I can identify letters and letter sounds.

You need:

The letter **Zz** makes the sound you hear in words like:

zebra

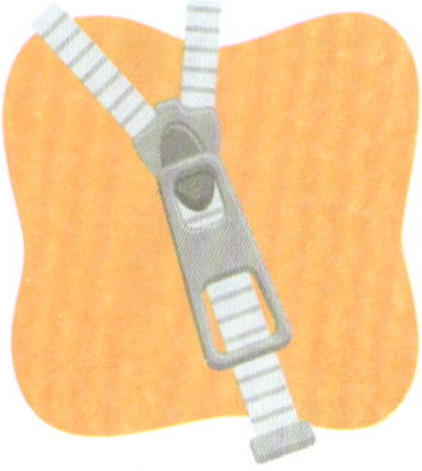

zipper

zoo

zero

zebu

Circle all of the **zebras** in the picture.

Got it! Not yet

You need:

Let's have some fun!

Connect the dots from **A** to **Z**.
Color the picture.

Got it! Not yet

I can write uppercase letters.

Remember:
Use the tripod grip!

Trace and write each letter.

A A B B

C C D D

E E F F

G G H H

I I J J

K K L L

Parent Tip:
Remind your child to start the letters at the top.

REUSABLE PAGE

I can write uppercase letters.

Trace and write each letter.

M M N N

O O P P

Q Q R R

S S T T

U U V V

W W X X

Y Y Z Z

REUSABLE PAGE

I can write lowercase letters.

Remember:
Use the tripod grip!

Trace and write each letter.

a a b b

c c d d

e e f f

g g h h

i i j j

k k l l

I can write lowercase letters.

REUSABLE PAGE

Trace and write each letter.

m m n n

o o p p

q q r r

s s t t

u u v v

w w x x

y y z z

Page 124

Page 125

Page 126

Page 127

HIP HIP HOORAY
KEEP IT UP!
AMAZING!!!
KEEP IT UP!
FLY HIGH
EXCELLENT
WAY TO GO!
YOU DID IT!
KEEP GOING!
GOOD JOB!
Rocking!

I can hold my scissors correctly.

You need:

Put your thumb through the small scissor handle.

Put your pointer and middle finger through the larger handle.

Hold the paper you want to cut in your other hand.

Cut away from you, not towards you!

Online Extra: To go to this activity, use your smartphone camera, hover over this code, and click on the link. Or go to: **anywhereteacher.com/qr/14161/11.**

Hold the paper on the edge. Cut along the dotted lines.

Got it! Not yet

I can cut lines.

Tell a story with the cut-out jellyfish.

I can cut lines.

You need:

Cut along the dotted lines.

Got it! Not yet

I can cut lines.

You need:

Tear out this page from the book.
Cut along the dotted lines.
These shapes will be used on page 7.

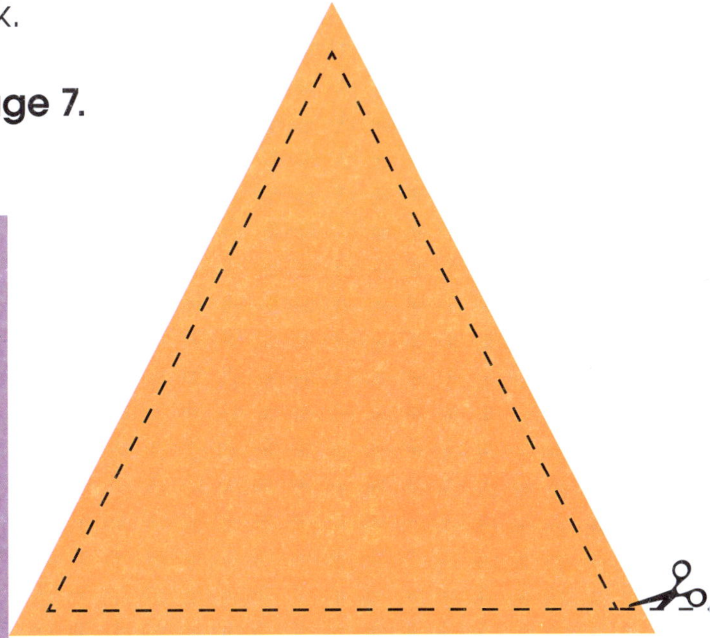

Got it! Not yet

I can match shapes.

You need:

Paste the shapes you just cut out to the matching spaces below.

Square

Circle

Triangle

Star

Got it! Not yet

Let's have some fun!

You need:

Connect the dots from **1** to **10**.
Color the picture.

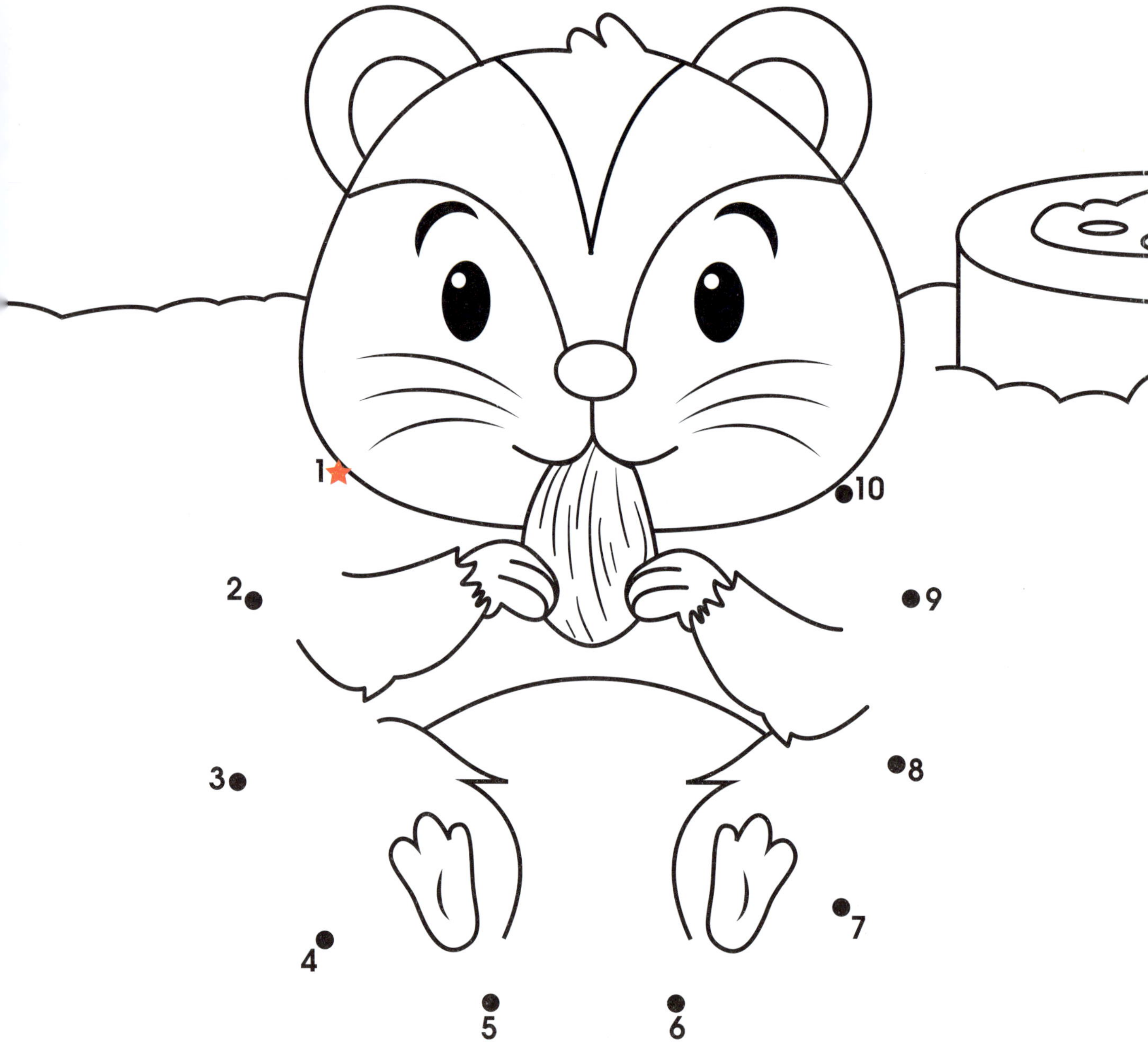

Got it! Not yet

I can get help from my parents to read this page.

Why is counting important?
Your child needs to be able to count accurately in order for them to add and subtract. They need this skill in order to do any mental math. Children also need to be able to understand that the last number they say indicates the number of objects they have. If you tell them to count the number of pennies and they count 1, 2, 3, they need to be able to then tell you "I have three pennies."

Counting Strategies

Common Mistakes
When your child counts make sure that they do not skip any objects or count an object twice. Give them helpful strategies like have them pull the item away from the pile to avoid counting it twice.

When counting out loud, make sure they are not skipping over numbers. This happens often when counting teen numbers: 11, 12, 13, 14, 16, 17, 18, 19, 20. Some may say my child can count to 20, but skips the number 15. None of the numbers matter past the first mistake, so you will need to correct this problem before it becomes a habit. The same thing goes for counting by tens to 100.

The Goal
Continue practicing with your preschooler to count to 20 (and beyond) before entering kindergarten.

I can start to understand that every number that I count matches only 1 object.

You need:

1

one

Trace and write the number **1**.

Circle 1 barn.

Color 1 airplane.

Draw 1 cloud.

Got it! Not yet

I can count a group of objects.

I know that the last number that I say is the total number of objects in the group.

You need:

Circle what there is only **1** of in the picture below.

Parent Tip:
When counting, touch each object as you are counting them.

Got it! Not yet

I can start to understand that every number that I count matches only 1 object.

You need:

2

two

Trace and write the number **2**.

Circle 2 fish.

Color 2 rings.

Draw 2 birds.

Got it!   Not yet

I can count a group of objects.

I know that the last number that I say is the total number of objects in the group.

You need:

Circle what there is only **2** of in the picture below.

Got it!   Not yet

I can start to understand that every number that I count matches only 1 object.

You need:

3

three

Trace and write the number **3**.

Circle 3 rabbits.

Color 3 cacti.

Draw 3 ants.

Got it! Not yet

You need:

I can count a group of objects.

I know that the last number that I say is the total number of objects in the group.

Circle what there is only **3** of in the picture below.

Got it! Not yet

I can start to understand that every number that I count matches only 1 object.

You need:

4

four

Trace and write the number **4**.

1 2 3

Circle **4** bows.

Color **4** buckets.

Draw **4** beach balls.

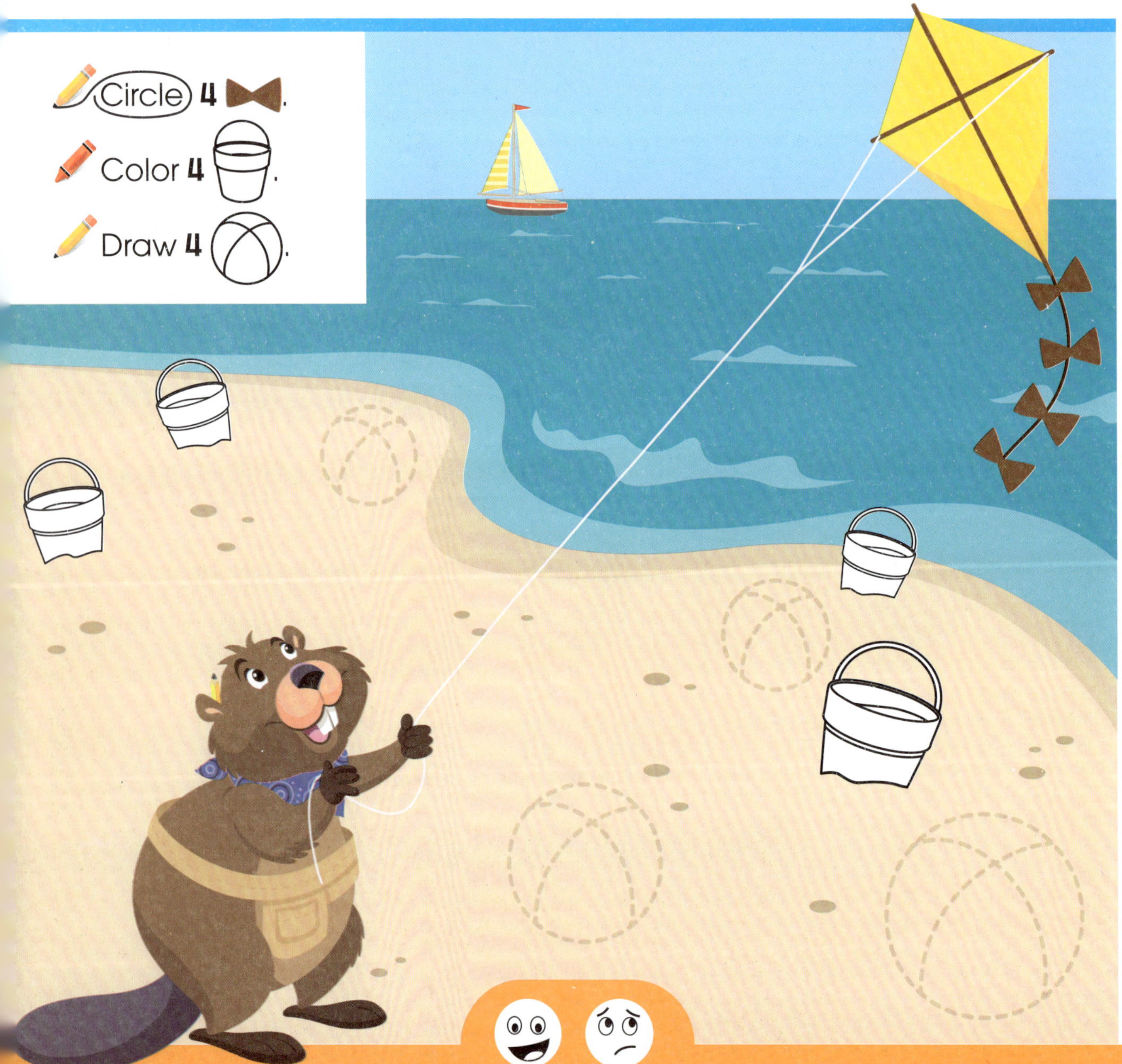

Got it! Not yet

I can count a group of objects.

I know that the last number that I say is the total number of objects in the group.

You need:

Circle what there is only **4** of in the picture below.

Got it! Not yet

You need:

I can start to understand that every number that I count matches only 1 object.

5

five

Trace and write the number **5**.

5 5

Circle **5** eyes.

Color **5** bats.

Draw **5** shells.

Got it! Not yet

I can count a group of objects.

I know that the last number that I say is the total number of objects in the group.

You need:

Circle what there is only **5** of in the picture below.

Got it! Not yet

Let's have some fun!

You need:

Color the scene.

1 = 2 = 3 = 4 = 5 =

Got it! Not yet

You need:

Let's have some fun!

Circle all of the .

Got it! Not yet

You need:

I can start to understand that every number that I count matches only 1 object.

6

six

Trace and write the number **6**.

Circle **6** acorns.

Color **6** leaves.

Draw **6** butterflies.

Got it! Not yet

You need:

I can count a group of objects.

I know that the last number that I say is the total number of objects in the group.

Circle what there is only **6** of in the picture below.

Got it! Not yet

You need:

I can start to understand that every number that I count matches only 1 object.

7

seven

Trace and write the number **7**.

7 7

Circle **7** fish.

Color **7** coins.

Draw **7** bubbles.

Got it! Not yet

I can count a group of objects.

I know that the last number that I say is the total number of objects in the group.

You need:

Circle what there is only 7 of in the picture below.

Got it! Not yet

I can start to understand that every number that I count matches only 1 object.

You need:

8

eight

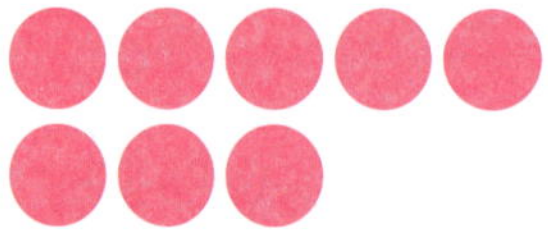

Trace and write the number **8**.

Circle **8** .

Color **8** .

Draw **8** .

Got it! Not yet

I can count a group of objects.

I know that the last number that I say is the total number of objects in the group.

You need:

Circle what there is only **8** of in the picture below.

Got it! Not yet

You need:

I can start to understand that every number that I count matches only 1 object.

9

nine

Trace and write the number **9**.

Circle **9** .

Color **9** .

Draw **9** .

Got it! Not yet

You need:

I can count a group of objects.

I know that the last number that I say is the total number of objects in the group.

Circle what there is only **9** of in the picture below.

Got it!   Not yet

You need:

I can start to understand that every number that I count matches only 1 object.

10

ten

Trace and write the number **10**.

10 10

Circle **10** frogs.

Color **10** rocks.

Draw **10** butterflies.

Got it! Not yet

I can count a group of objects.

I know that the last number that I say is the total number of objects in the group.

You need:

Circle what there is only **10** of in the picture below.

Got it! Not yet

Let's have some fun!

You need:

Draw a line from the cow through the numbers **0-10** to the barn.

Got it! Not yet

Let's have some fun!

You need:

Circle the **10**  in the scene.

Got it! Not yet

I can recognize basic emotions.

There are many emotions you may feel.

afraid

confused

disgusted

embarrassed

excited

happy

mad

proud

sad

silly

surprised

worried

Online Extra:
To go to this activity, use your smartphone camera, hover over this code, and click on the link. Or go to: **anywhereteacher.com/qr/14161/12.**

I can recognize basic emotions.

You need:

Circle the emotion that matches the picture.

Got it! Not yet

I can recognize basic emotions.

You need:

Circle the emotion that matches the picture.

Got it! Not yet

I can recognize basic emotions.

Circle the emotion that matches the picture.

Got it! Not yet

You need:

I can recognize basic emotions.

Draw a line between the matching emotions.

Got it! Not yet

I can start to write my numbers 0-10.

Trace the numbers **0** to **4**.

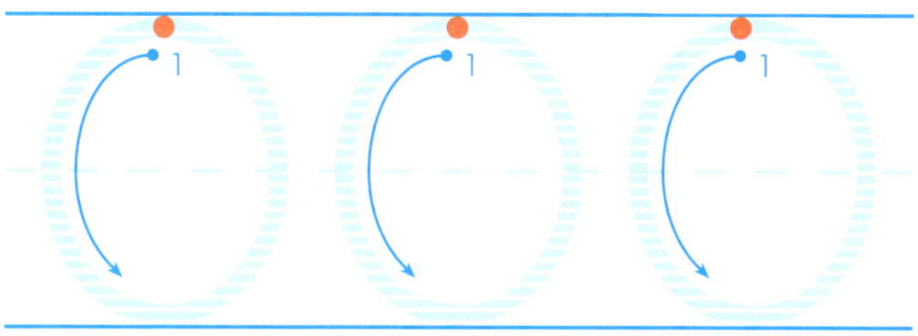

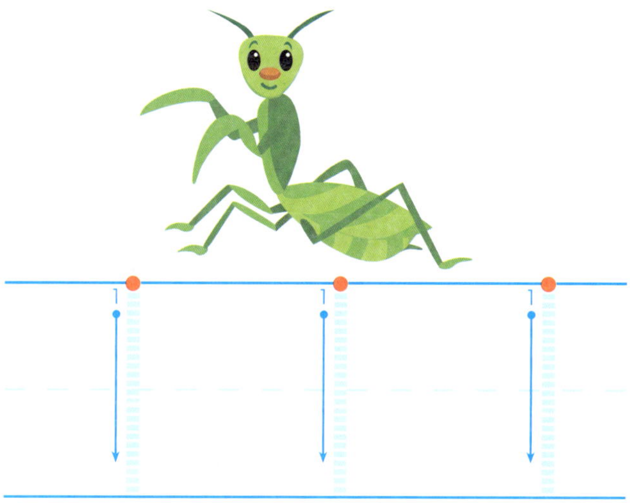

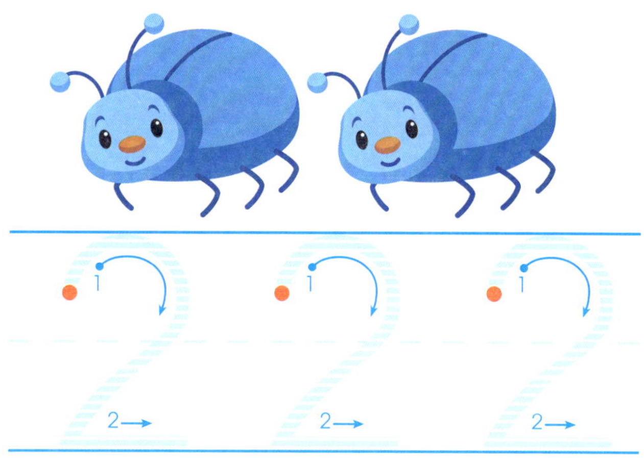

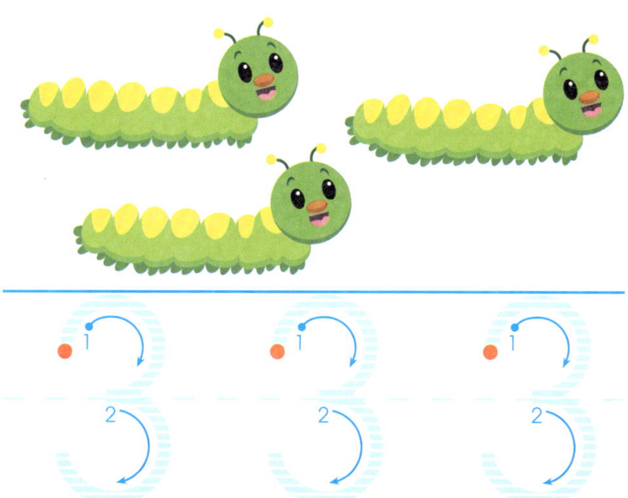

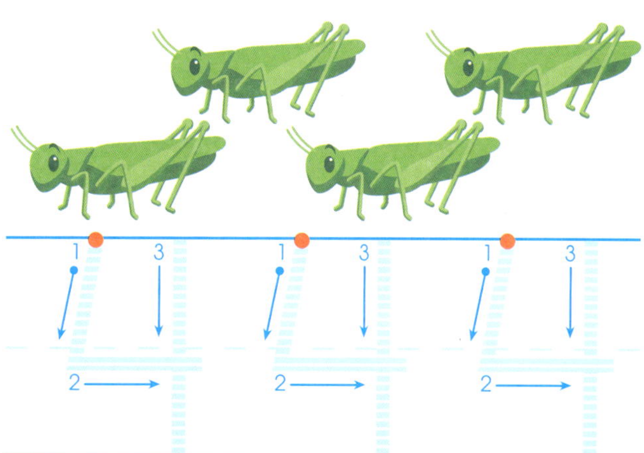

Got it! Not yet

REUSABLE PAGE

I can start to write my numbers 0-10.

Trace the numbers **5** to **10**.

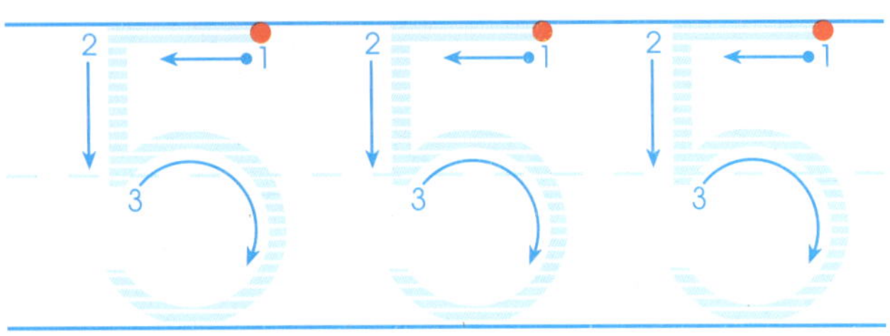

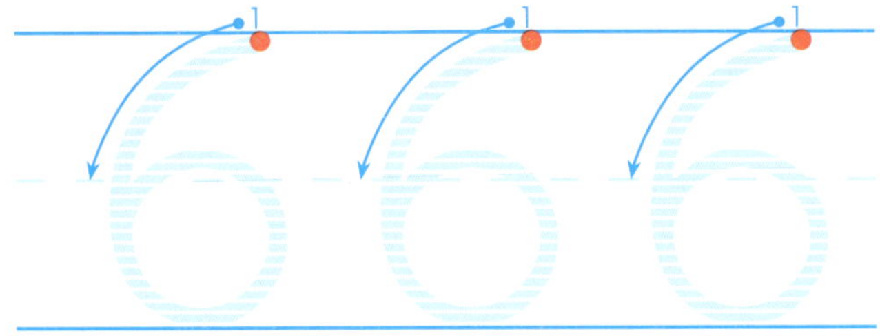

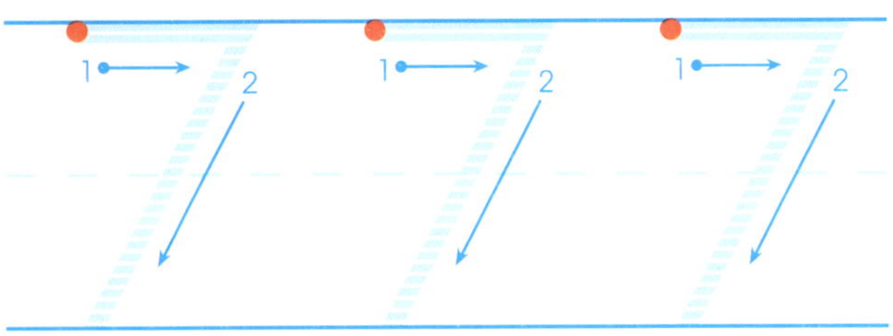

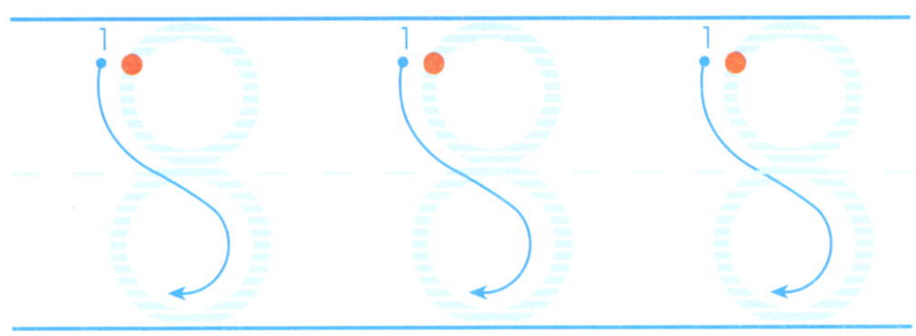

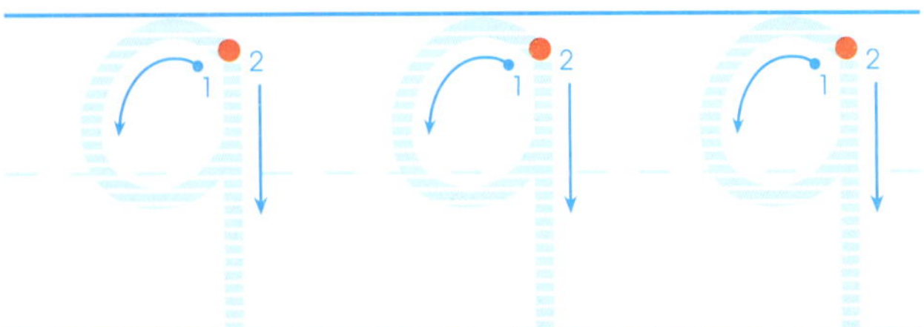

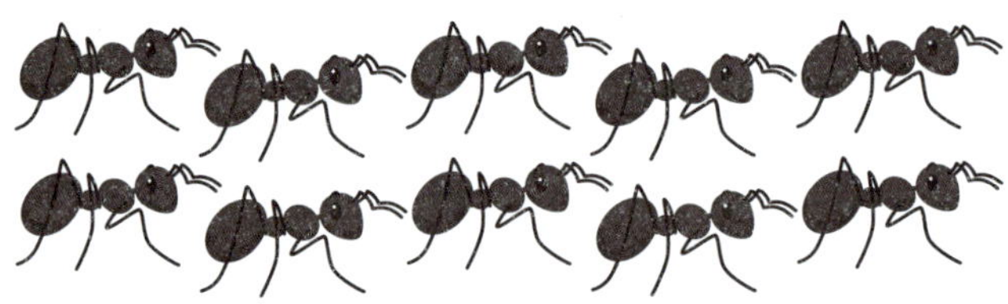

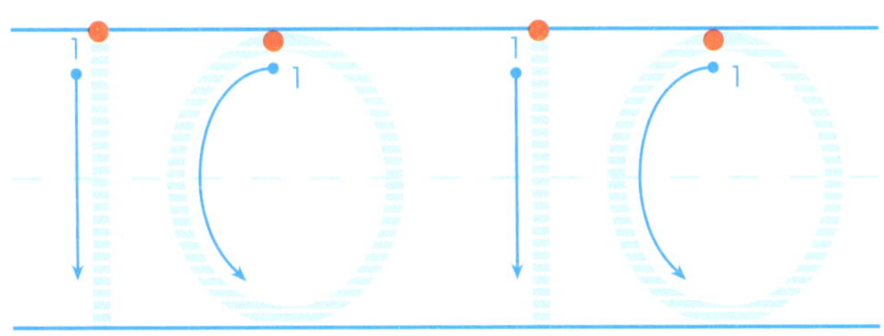

Got it! Not yet

I can start to read my numbers 0-10.

You need:

Connect the dots from **1** to **10**.
Color the picture.

Got it! Not yet

I can start to read my numbers 0-10.

You need:

Connect the dots from **1** to **10**.
Color the picture.

Got it! Not yet

I can hear and match beginning sounds in words.

You need:

bear

bee

Circle the picture that begins with the **same sound** as the first one.

monkey

tree

mouse

bird

banana

frog

pig

book

pear

Got it! Not yet

I can hear and match beginning sounds in words.

You need: pencil

Circle the picture that begins with the **same sound** as the first one.

turkey

turtle

lemon

ladder

hamburger

lion

nest

hat

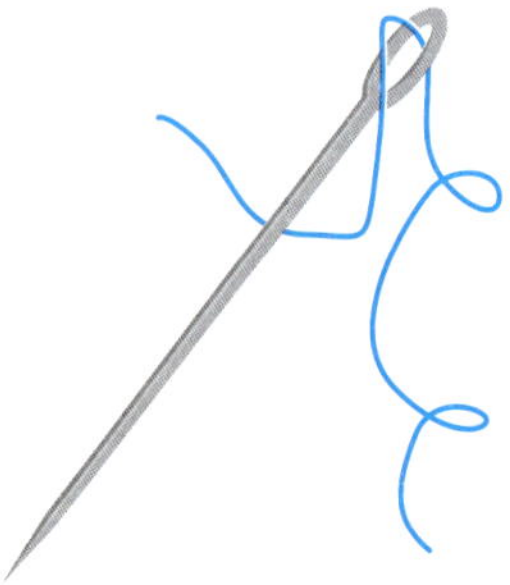
needle

dog

doll

car

Got it! Not yet

You need:

I can hear and match beginning sounds in words.

Circle the picture that begins with the **same sound** as the first one.

Got it! Not yet

You need:

I can hear and match beginning sounds in words.

Circle the picture that begins with the **same sound** as the first one.

  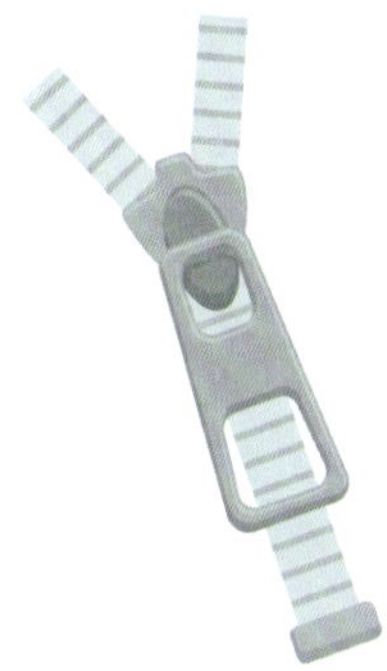

Got it! Not yet

Let's have some fun!

You need:

Circle all of the .

Got it! Not yet

I can hear and match beginning sounds in words.

Say the name of each picture.

Circle the pictures that have the same beginning sound.

Got it! Not yet

You need:

I can hear and match beginning sounds in words.

Say the name of each picture.

Circle the pictures that have the same beginning sound.

Got it! Not yet

You need:

I can hear and match beginning sounds in words.

Say the name of each picture.

Circle the pictures that begin with the **same sound**.

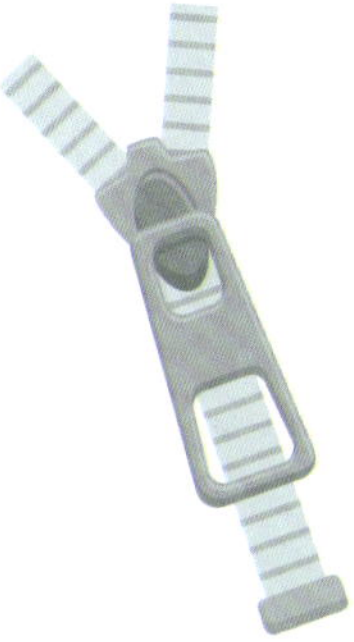

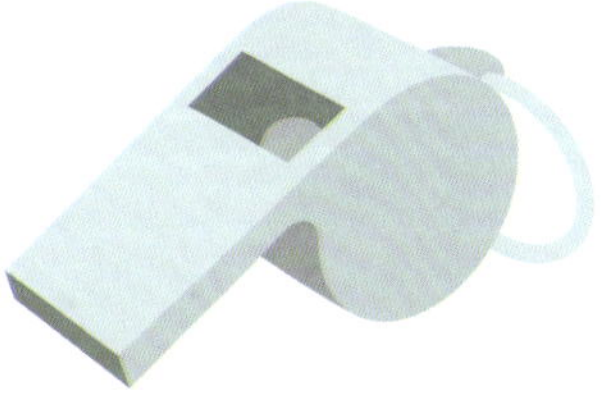

Got it! Not yet

You need:

I can hear and match beginning sounds in words.

Say the name of each picture.

Circle the pictures that begin with the **same sound**.

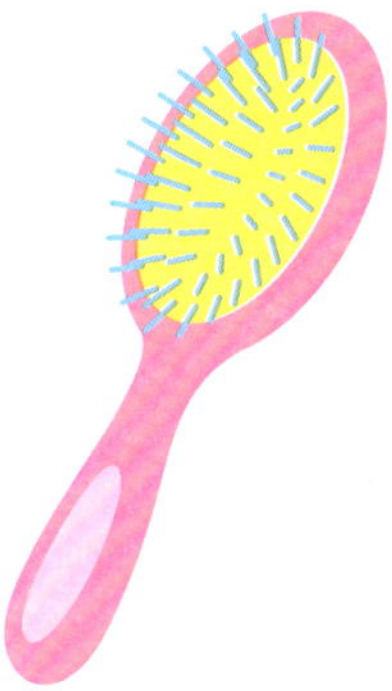

Got it! Not yet

You need:

I can hear and match beginning sounds in words.

Say the name of each picture.
Circle the letter that begins each word.

U S T

A B C

G H I

D E F

O P Q

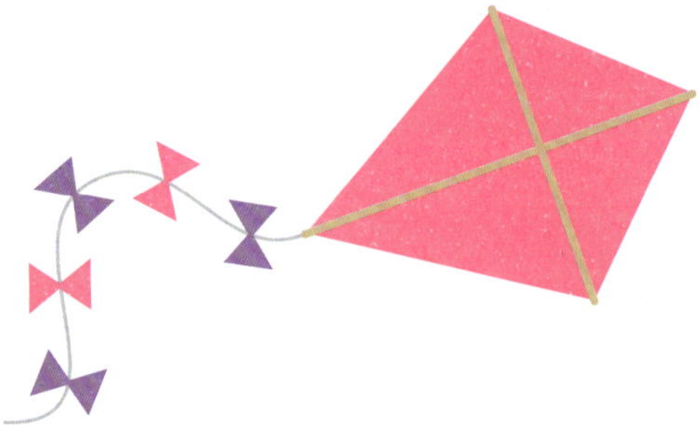

J K L

Got it! Not yet

You need:

I can hear and match beginning sounds in words.

Say the name of each picture.
Circle the letter that begins each word.

L M N

X Y Z

C D E

M N O

L M N

J K L

Got it! Not yet

Let's have some fun!

You need:

Draw a line from the  to the .

Got it!

Not yet

I can make or draw shapes.

You need:

Draw lines between the shapes that match.

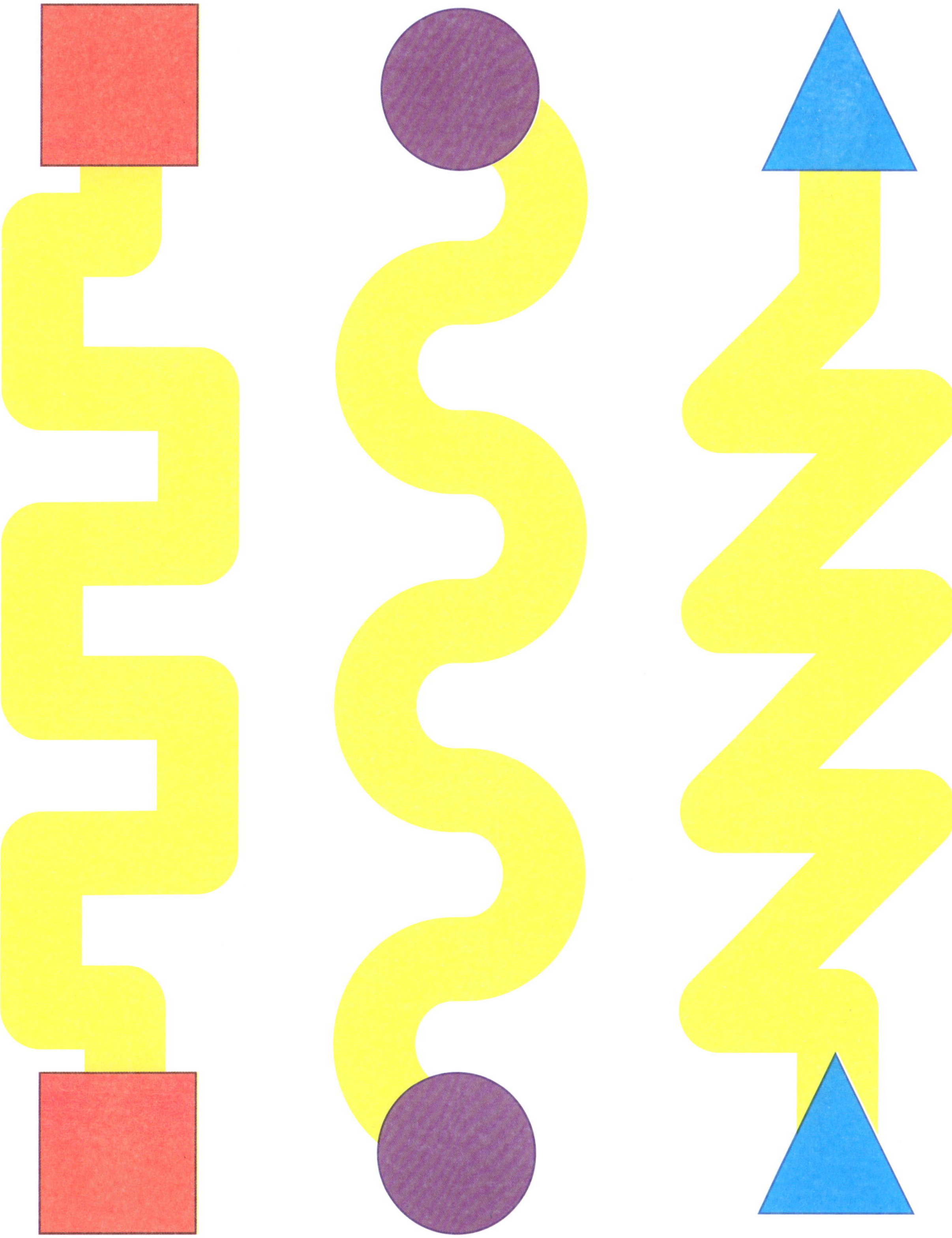

Got it! Not yet

You need:

I can make or draw shapes.

This is a **square**.

Trace the squares.
Start at the red dot (●).

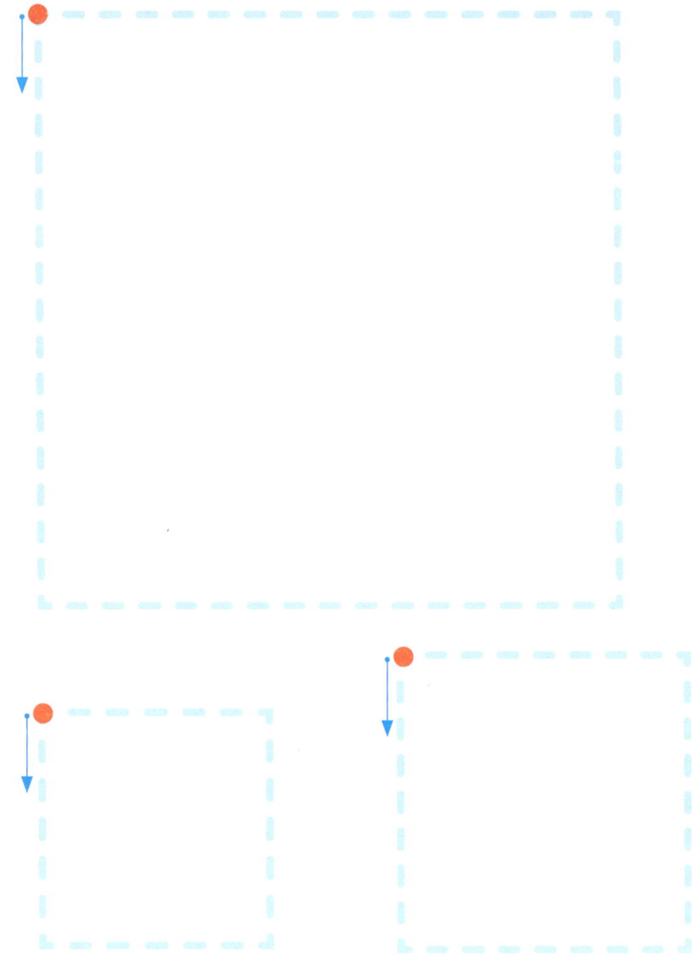

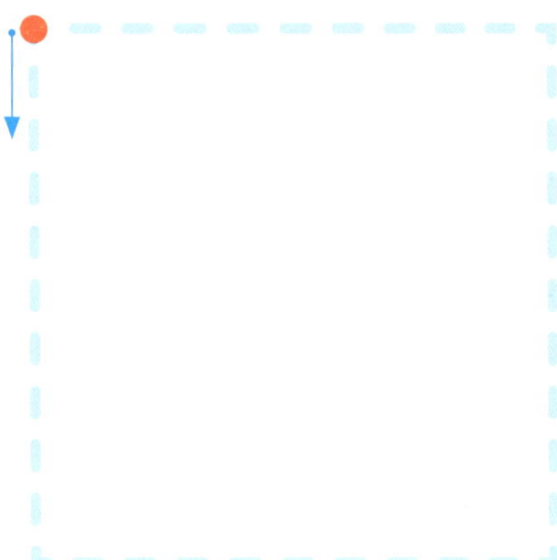

Color the **squares**.

Got it! Not yet

You need:

I can make or draw shapes.

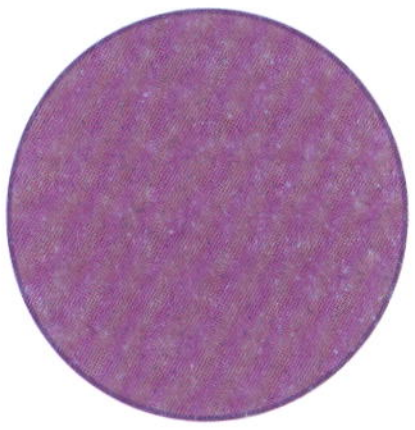

This is a **circle**.

Trace the circles.
Start at the red dot (●).

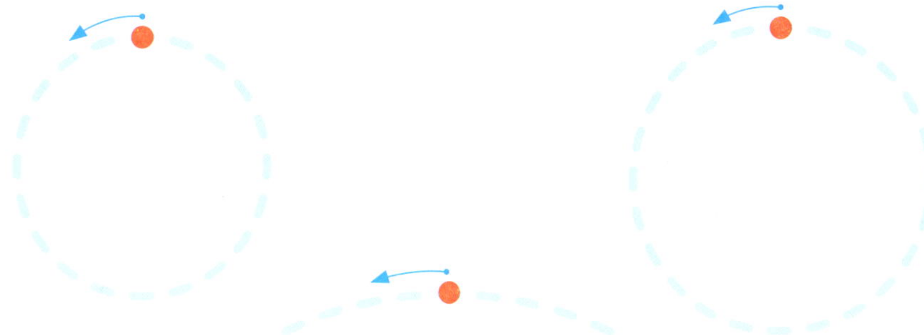

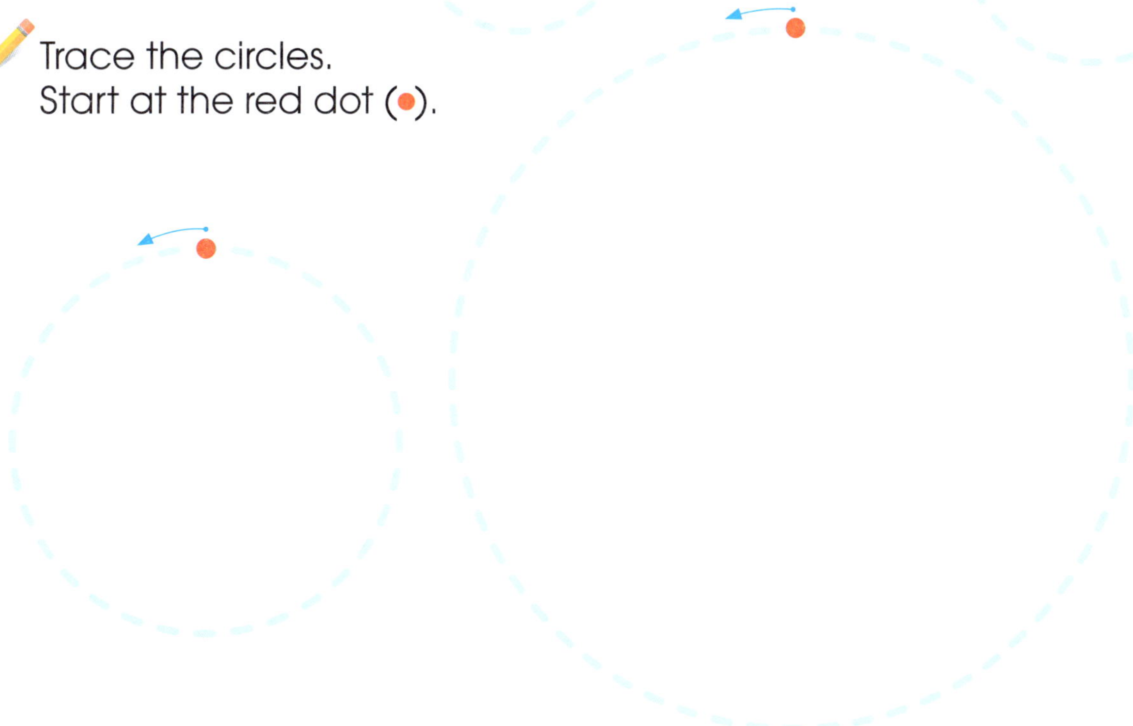

Color the **circles**.

Got it! Not yet

I can make or draw shapes.

You need:

This is a **triangle**.

Trace the triangles.
Start at the red dot (●).

Color the **triangles**.

Got it! Not yet

I can make or draw shapes.

You need:

Draw lines between the shapes that match.

Got it! Not yet

I can make or draw shapes.

You need:

This is a **diamond**.

Trace the diamonds.
Start at the red dot (●).

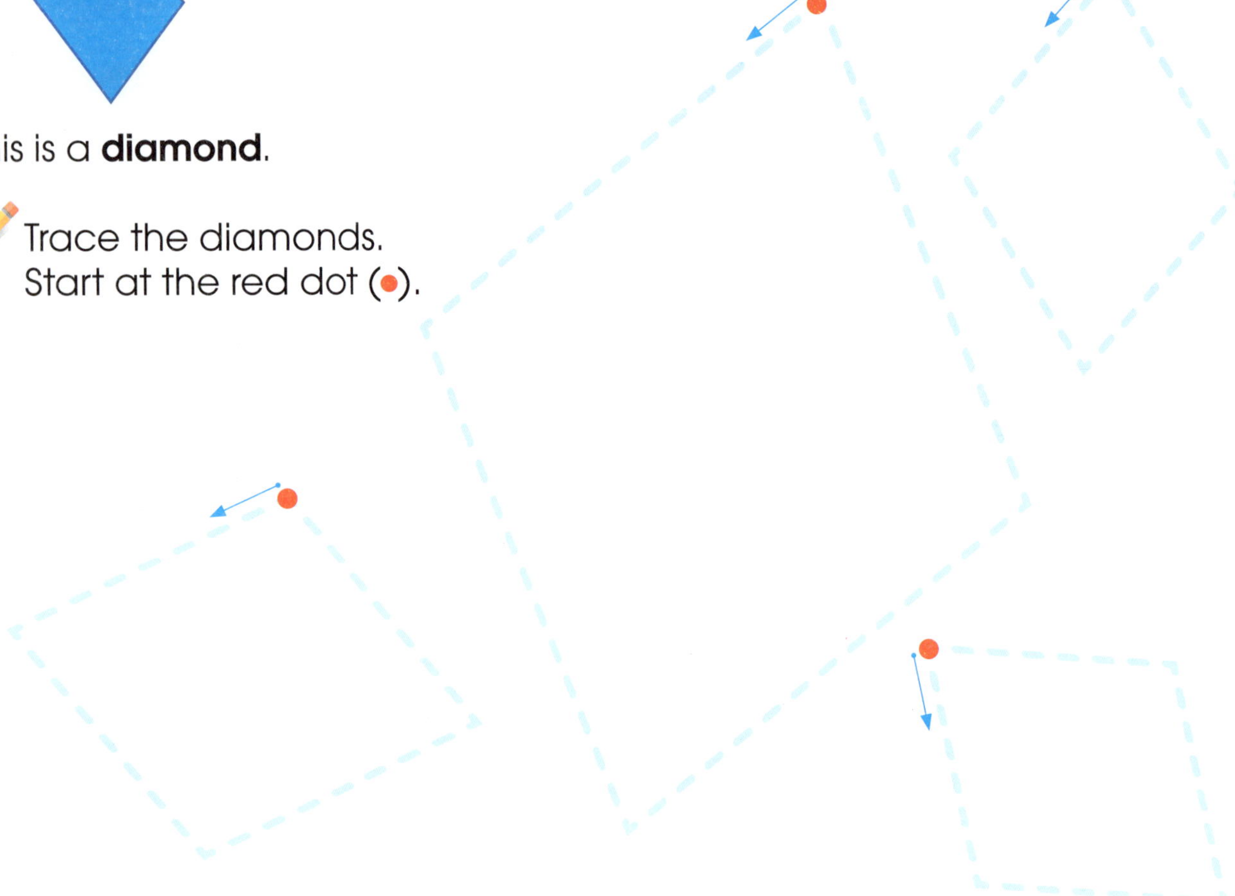

Color the **diamonds**.

Got it! Not yet

I can make or draw shapes.

You need:

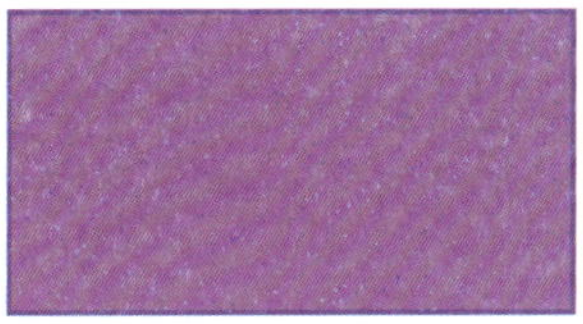

This is a **rectangle**.

Trace the rectangles.
Start at the red dot (●).

Color the **rectangles**.

Got it! Not yet

I can make or draw shapes.

You need:

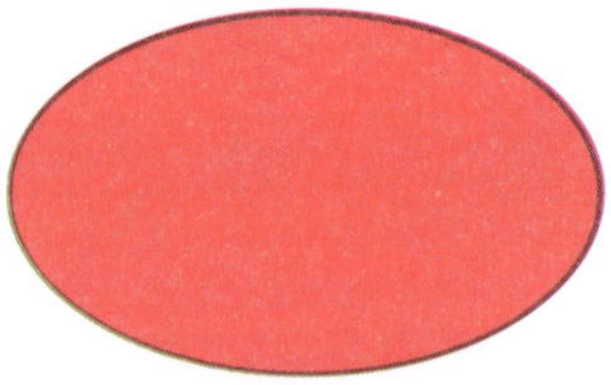

This is an **oval**.

Trace the ovals.
Start at the red dot (●).

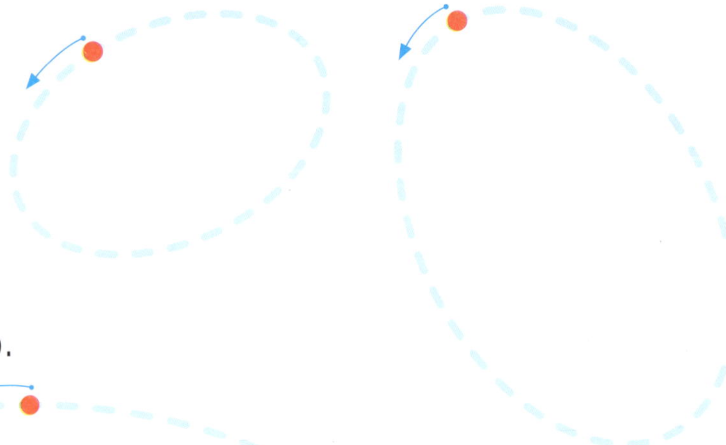

Color the **ovals**.

Got it! Not yet

You need:

I can sort shapes.

Draw lines to match the pictures to the shapes.

circle

square

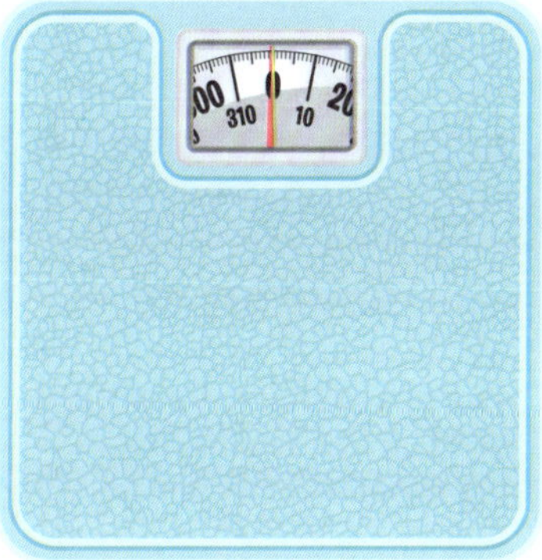

triangle

Got it!　Not yet

You need:

I can sort shapes.

Draw lines to match the pictures to the shapes.

Got it! Not yet

You need:

I can understand that one group of objects can be sorted lots of different ways and explain why I sorted them that way.

Use the shape press-out pieces, and sort them into the box below. For example, you could sort them by **size**, **shape**, or **color**.

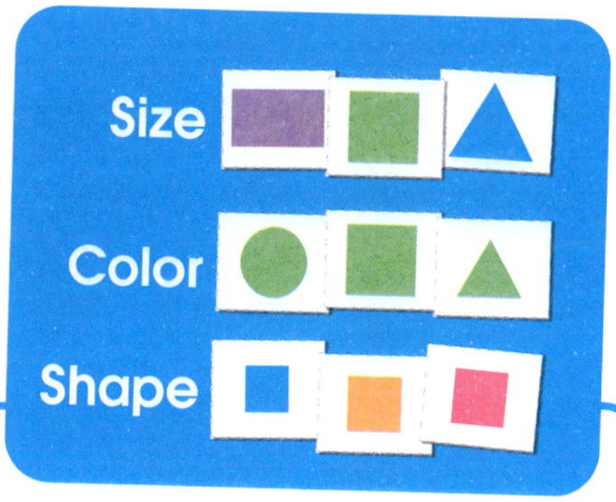

Parent Tip:
Have your child sort their shapes here, and then explain why they sorted the way they did.

Got it! Not yet

Let's have some fun!

You need:

Color the scene.

1 = 2 = 3 = 4 = 5 =

Got it! Not yet

REUSABLE PAGE

I can name my own emotions.

Circle how you feel right now:

happy

sad

Draw a picture of you and how you feel right now.

Parent Tip:
Have your child do this page frequently to notice emotions change.

Got it! Not yet

I can match most uppercase and lowercase letters together.

Draw a line from each uppercase letter to the matching lowercase letter.

E A B J

a e j b

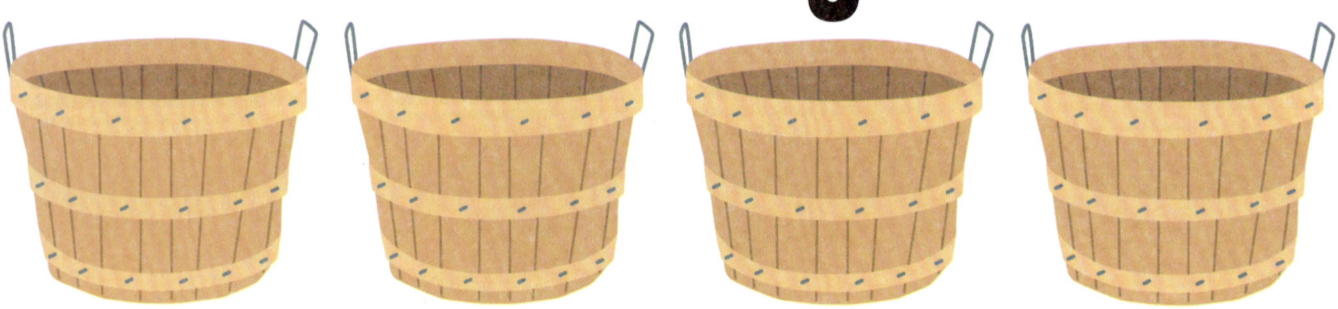

Got it! Not yet

You need:

I can match most uppercase and lowercase letters together.

Draw a line from each uppercase letter to the matching lowercase letter.

O K M Q

q m o k

Got it! Not yet

You need:

I can match most uppercase and lowercase letters together.

Draw a line from each uppercase letter to the matching lowercase letter.

D N P L

n l d p

Got it! Not yet

You need:

I can match most uppercase and lowercase letters together.

Draw a line from each uppercase letter to the matching lowercase letter.

T H Z F

z f t h

Got it! Not yet

You need:

I can match most uppercase and lowercase letters together.

Draw a line from each uppercase letter to the matching lowercase letter.

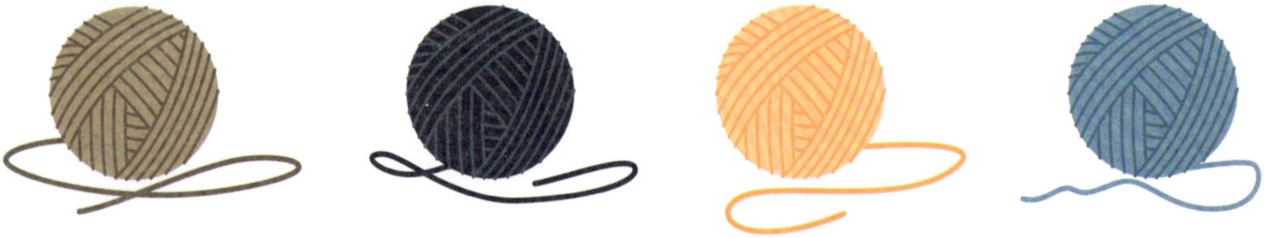

G R S I

r s g i

Got it! Not yet

You need:

I can match most uppercase and lowercase letters together.

Draw a line from each uppercase letter to the matching lowercase letter.

W U V X

v w x u

Parent Tip:
Use the letter press-out pieces to match uppercase and lowercase letters.

Got it! Not yet

You need:

I can identify uppercase and lowercase letters.

Circle the letters that match the first letters in each row.

Ff T F f P e F

Gg G O g q G b

Kk X h K k Y K

Ll L i l T L I

Mm M m u N v M

Got it! Not yet

You need:

I can identify uppercase and lowercase letters.

Circle the letters that match the first letters in each row.

Zz N M Z z v Z

Yy X Y y K Z y

Jj j G U J j g

Hh H h b H E h

Bb E b B d B P

Got it! Not yet

Parent Tip:
Check the **Bb** row.

You need:

I can identify uppercase and lowercase letters.

Circle the letters that match the first letters in each row.

Cc O c C a c Q

Aa V A a A K W

Qq Q O C q q p

Dd B d D b d P

Ee F e E o g e

Parent Tip: Check the **Qq** and **Dd** rows.

Got it! Not yet

You need:

I can identify uppercase and lowercase letters.

Circle the letters that match the first letters in each row.

Nn	M	N	n	h	n	m
Ii	L	i	T	I	i	j
Pp	p	b	P	q	g	p
Uu	V	u	J	u	U	n
Tt	t	F	T	H	L	t

Got it! Not yet

I can write my alphabet.

You need:

Trace the **letters** of the alphabet.

A B C D E

F G H I J K

L M N O P

Q R S T U

V W X Y Z

Got it! Not yet

I can write my alphabet.

You need:

Trace the **letters** of the alphabet.

a b c d e

f g h i j k

l m n o p

q r s t u

v w x y z

Got it! Not yet

I can write my own name.

Remember:
Use the tripod grip!

You need:

Ask a grown-up to write your first name.

Practice writing your name.

Got it!   Not yet

Parent Tip:
Check the letter formations to make sure your child is writing their name properly. Make sure their name is in proper case.

Let's have some fun!

You need:

Connect the dots from **A** to **Z**.
Color the picture.

Got it! Not yet

I can see and match number symbols to a group of objects.

You need:

Count how many boxes are filled in.

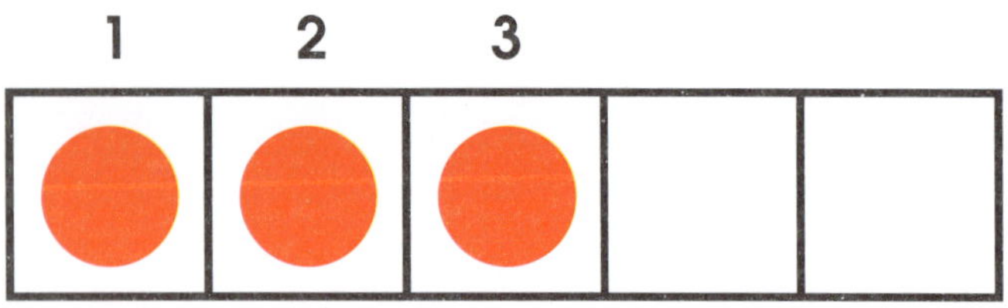

2 (3) 5

Count how many.
Circle the number.

1 2 3 4 5

1 2 3 4 5

1 2 3 4 5

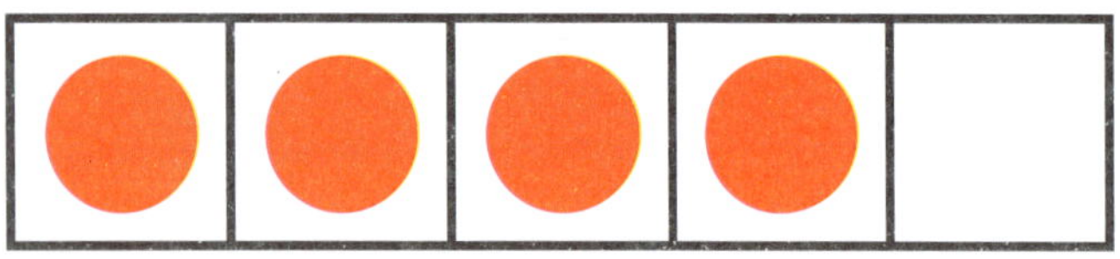

1 2 3 4 5

1 2 3 4 5

Got it! Not yet

You need:

I can see and match number symbols to a group of objects.

Read the number and color that many dots.
The first one is done for you.

1 ●○○○○

2 ○○○○○

3 ○○○○○

4 ○○○○○

5 ○○○○○

Got it! Not yet

You need:

I can see and match number symbols to a group of objects.

Read the number and color that many dots.

3 ○ ○ ○ ○ ○

4 ○ ○ ○ ○ ○

1 ○ ○ ○ ○ ○

5 ○ ○ ○ ○ ○

2 ○ ○ ○ ○ ○

Got it! Not yet

You need:

I can see and match number symbols to a group of objects.

Read the number and color that many dots.

2

1

3

4

5

Got it! Not yet

You need:

I can compare two groups of objects.

 is the **same** amount as .

Circle the group that shows the **same** number as the first one in each row.

Got it! Not yet

I can compare two groups of objects.

You need:

5 is **more than** 4.

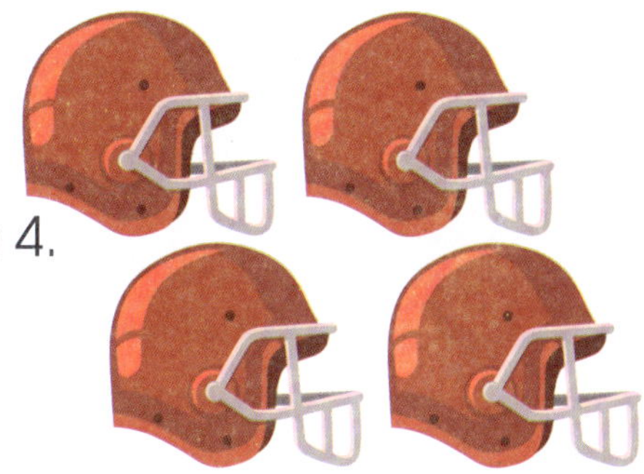

Circle the group that shows **more** in each row.

Got it! Not yet

I can compare two groups of objects.

You need:

2 is **less than** 4.

Circle the group that shows **less** in each row.

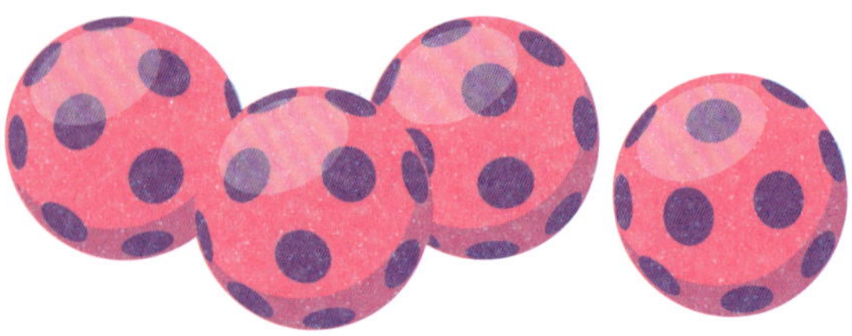

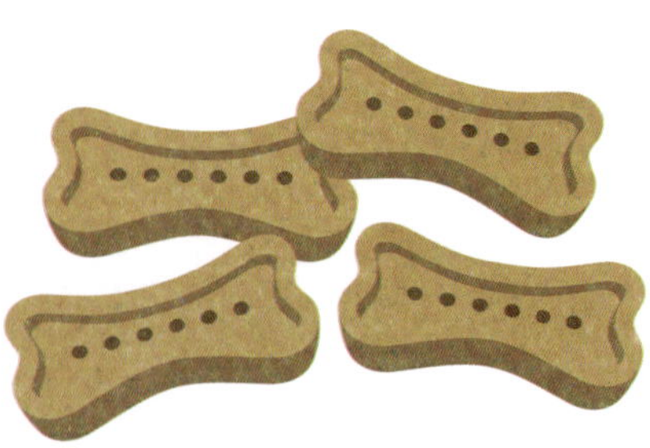

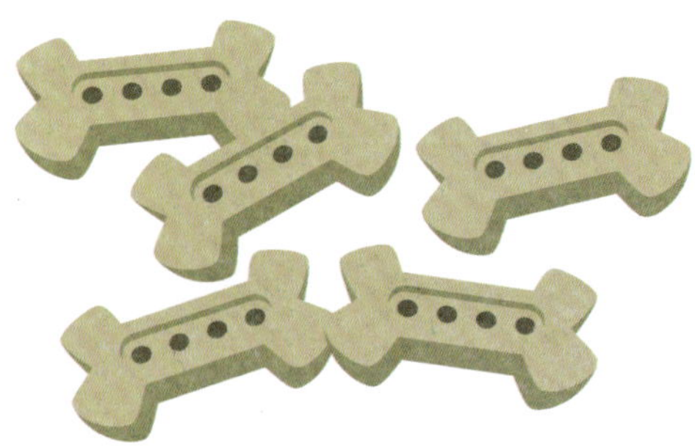

Got it! Not yet

You need:

I can sort groups of objects.

Draw a line to match the groups of the same number of animals.

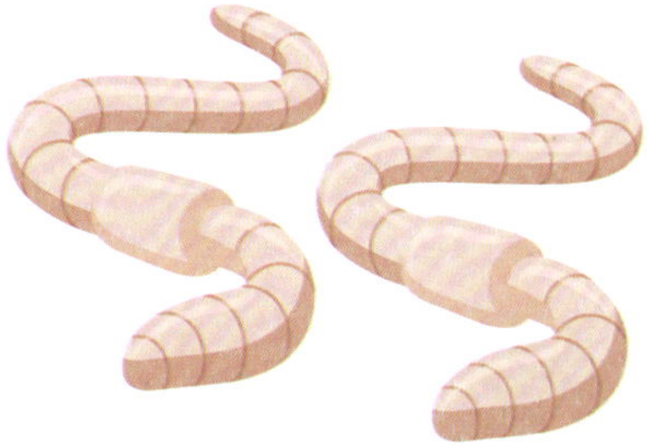

Got it!   Not yet

You need:

I can hear the ending sounds in words.

Say the name of each picture.

Circle the pictures in each row that end with the **same sound**.

Got it! Not yet

I can hear the ending sounds in words.

You need:

Say the name of each picture.
Circle the pictures in each row that end with the **same sound**.

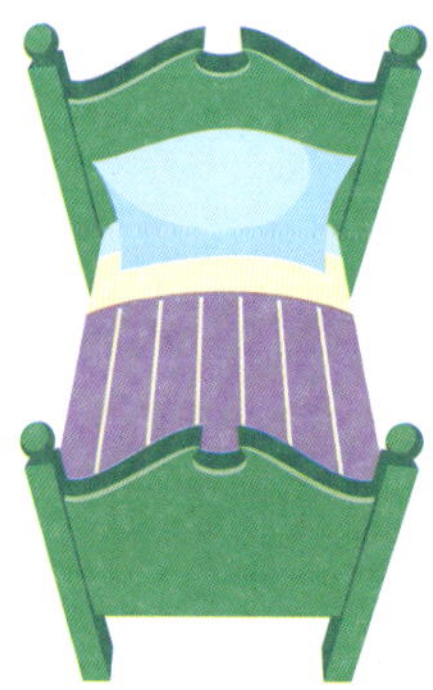

Got it! Not yet

Let's have some fun!

You need:

Circle what is different between **picture A** and **picture B**.

Picture A

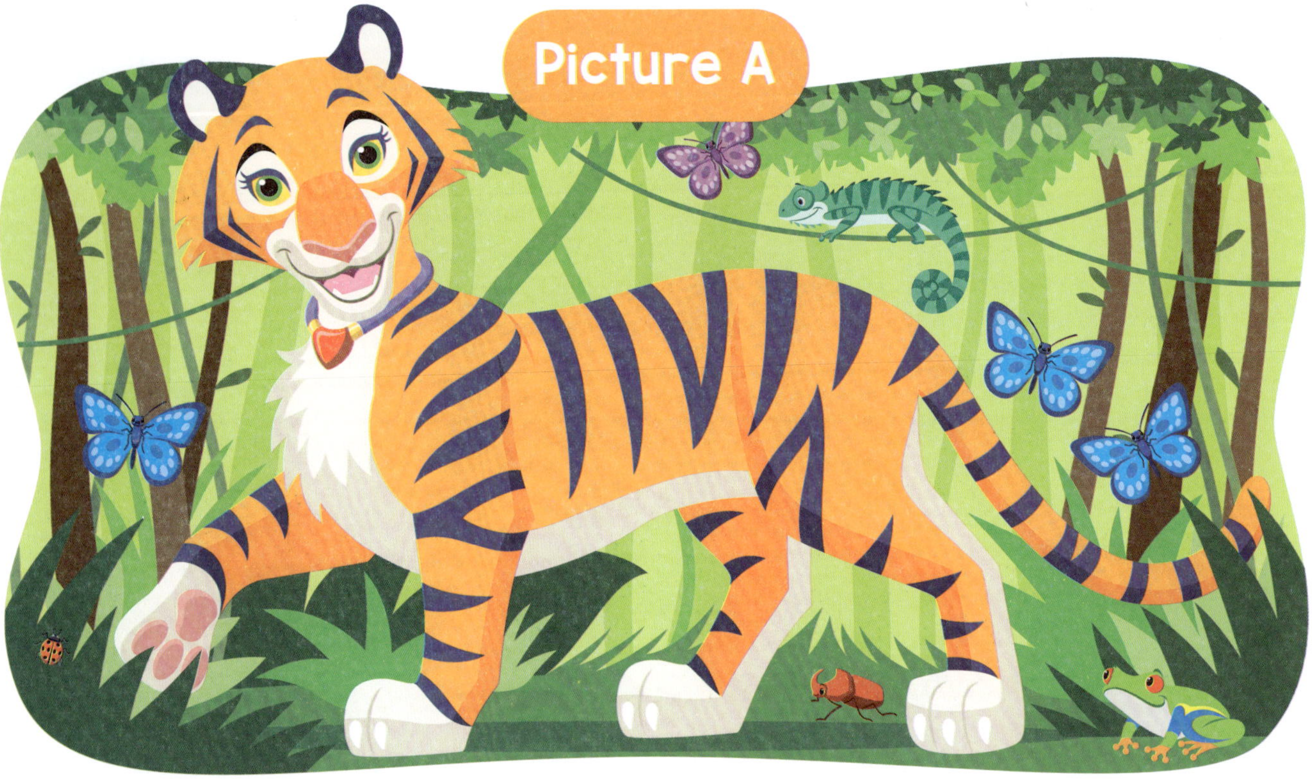

Picture B

Got it! Not yet

I can recognize and describe patterns.

You need:

Draw and color the shape to finish each pattern.
The first one is done for you.

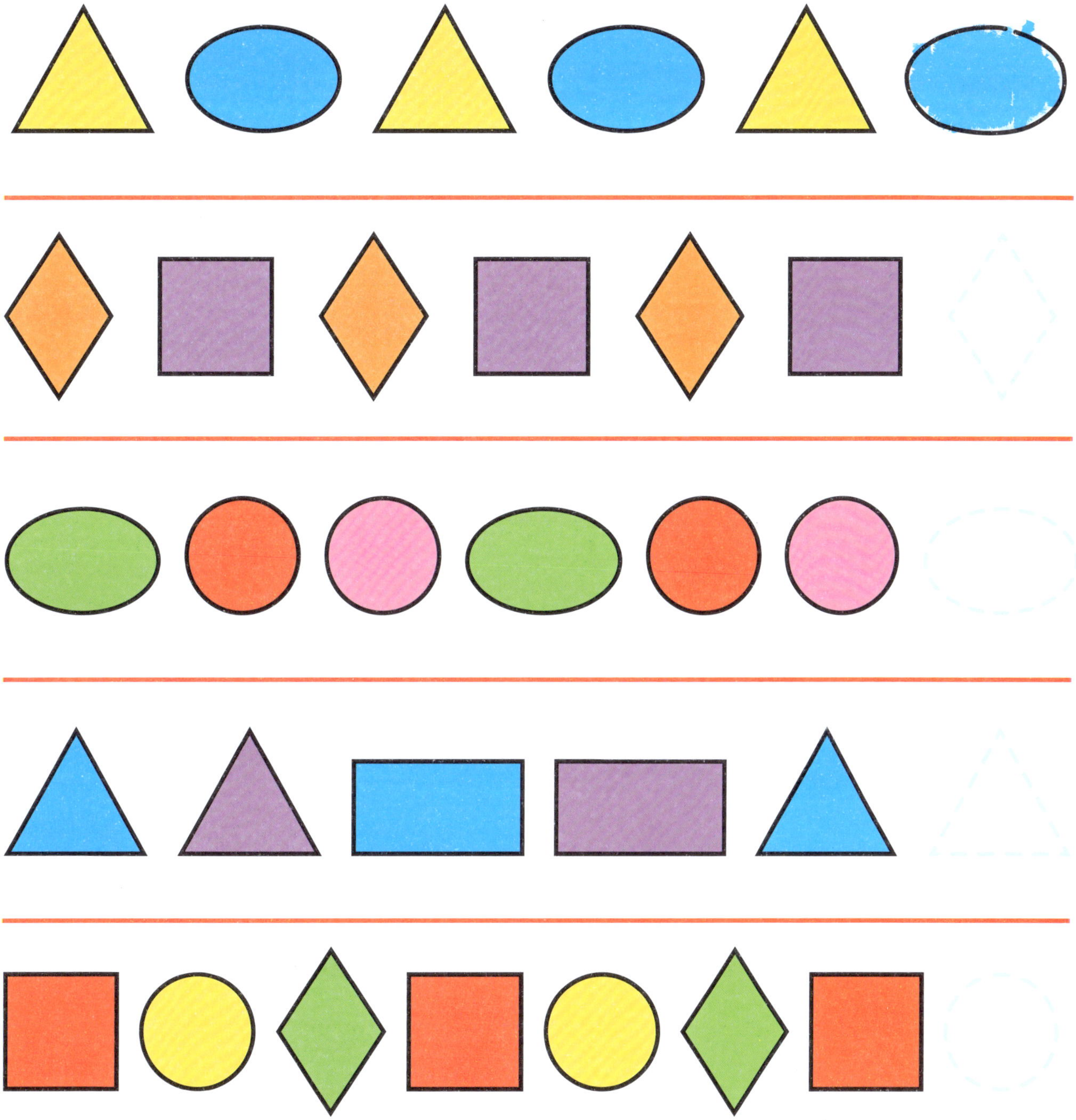

Parent Tip:
Ask your child, "What is the pattern?" Encourage your child to describe the pattern using colors, numbers, shapes, or any other attributes.

Got it! Not yet

You need:

I can copy patterns out of objects and pictures.

Use the press-out shape pieces to finish the pattens.

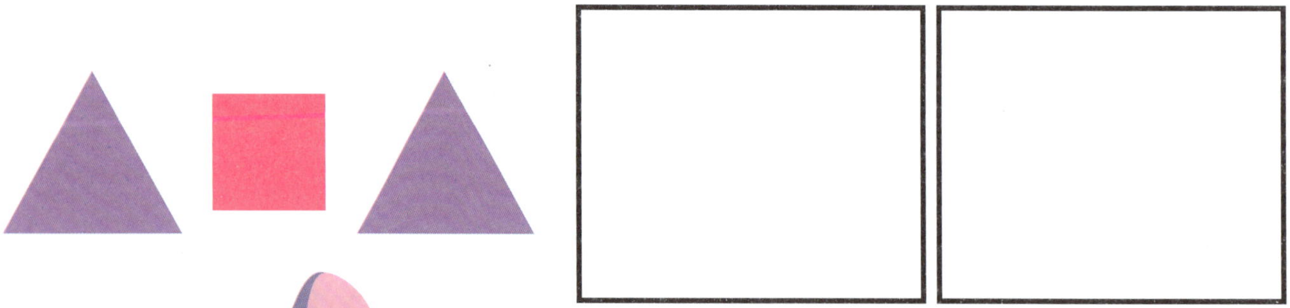

Parent Tip:
Encourage your child to describe the pattern using colors, numbers, shapes, or any other attributes.

Got it! Not yet

You need:

I can copy patterns out of objects and pictures.

Color the pictures to match the pattern.

Got it! Not yet

I can find patterns in the real world.

You need:

Circle all of the patterns you can find in the scene.

Got it! Not yet

You need:

Let's have some fun!

Draw a line from the  to the .

Got it! Not yet

You need:

I can be aware of other people's emotions.

Read the story.

You see Sam knock down Sarah's tower. Sarah starts to cry.

What would you do if someone knocked down your tower? Draw a picture.

Got it! Not yet

I can recognize my own emotions.

You need:

Read the picture story.

Circle how this makes you feel.

sad

happy

mad

confused

Got it! Not yet

You need:

I can control the way I impact other people's emotions.

Read the picture story.

Circle what you would do.

Got it! Not yet

I can control the way I impact other people's emotions.

You need:

Read the picture story.

Circle how the story makes you feel.

happy sad mad confused

Circle what you would do.

Got it! Not yet

I can describe a shape by talking about its corners and sides.

You need:

A **side** is a straight line that is part of a shape.
A **corner** is where two sides meet.

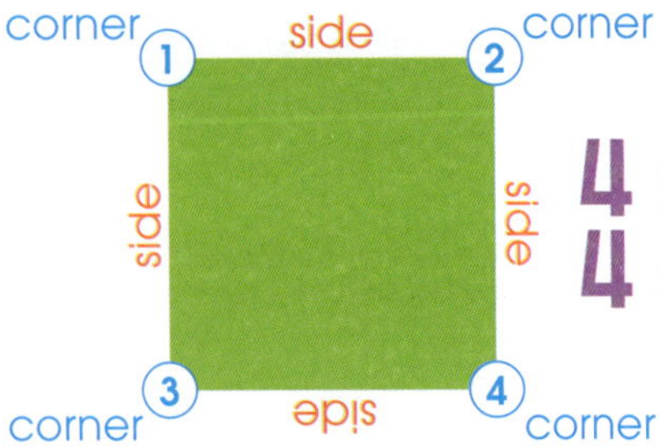

4 sides
4 corners

0 sides
0 corners

A circle has no sides and no corners.

Trace each shape.
Answer the questions.

How many corners? **4** **5**

How many sides? **4** **5**

How many corners? **0** **1**

How many sides? **0** **1**

How many corners? **3** **4**

How many sides? **3** **4**

How many corners? **1** **3**

How many sides? **1** **3**

Got it! Not yet

You need:

I can describe a shape by talking about its corners and sides.

Spread out the shape press-out pieces in front of you.
Count the number of sides on each shape.
Sort the shapes into the three groups below.

4 sides

0 sides

3 sides

Got it! Not yet

Let's have some fun!

You need:

Color the scene.

1 = 2 = 3 = 4 = 5 =

Got it! Not yet

You need:

Let's have some fun!

Circle all of the  you can find.

Got it! Not yet

You need:

I can hear rhymes.

Circle the picture that **rhymes** with the first one.

Got it!   Not yet

You need:

I can hear rhymes.

Say the names of the pictures in each group.
Do the pictures rhyme?
Circle yes or no.

Got it! Not yet

I can find and match rhymes.

You need:

Draw a line between the pictures in each group that rhyme.

Got it! Not yet

I can find and match rhymes.

You need:

Look at each row to see if the pictures rhyme with the first one.
Circle yes or no.

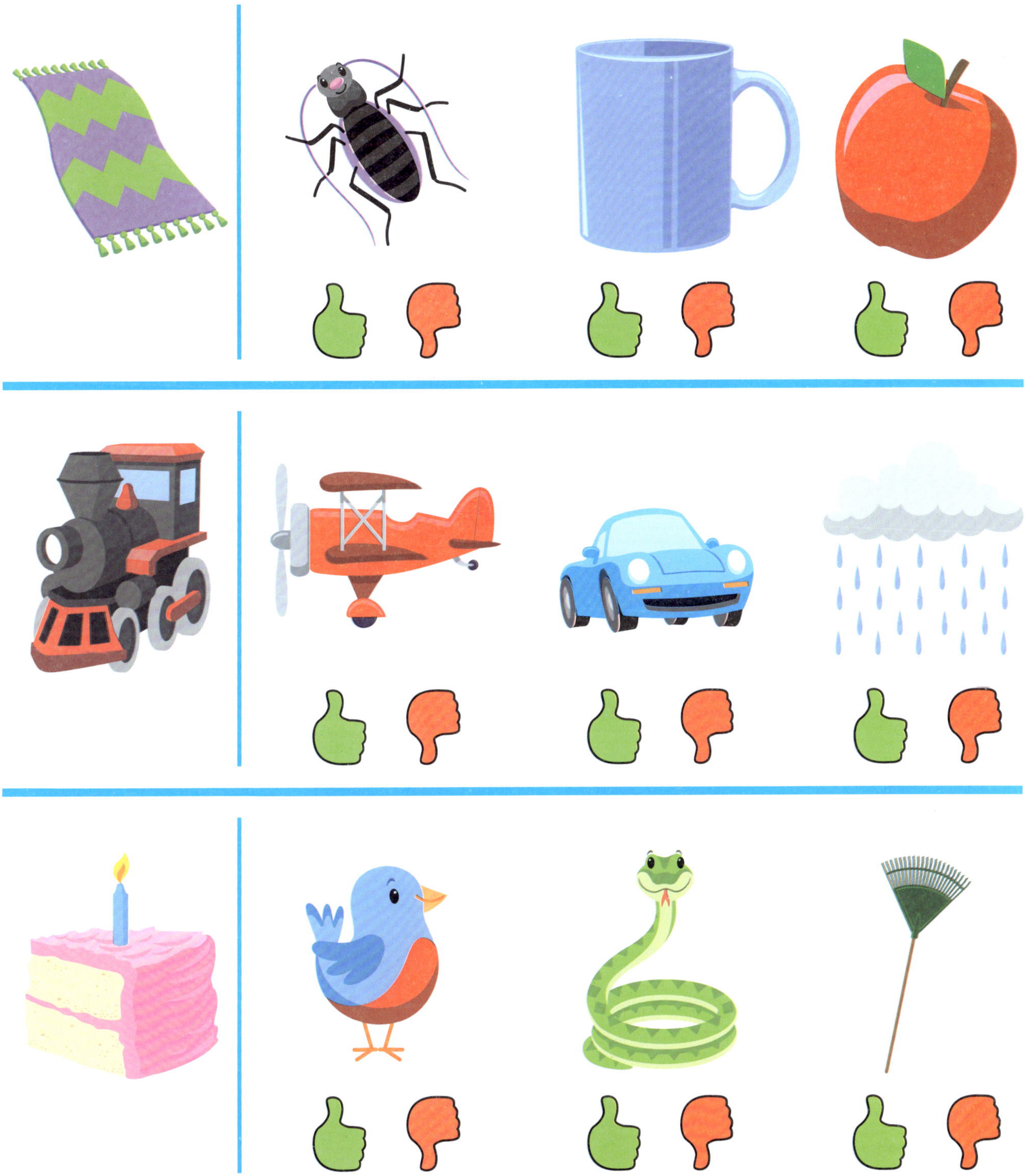

Got it! Not yet

You need:

I can find and match rhymes.

Write the missing letter(s) to make a word that rhymes with the first one.
Draw a picture of that word.

bat ___at

frog ___og

Got it! Not yet

You need:

Let's have some fun!

Circle what is different between **picture A** and **picture B**.

Picture A

Picture B

Got it! Not yet

I can put together a broken word.

Cut out the letters on the next page. Place the letters in the spaces to make the word that matches each picture.

Example: 

Parent Tip:
Say the beginning sound, and then say the rest of the word.

You need:

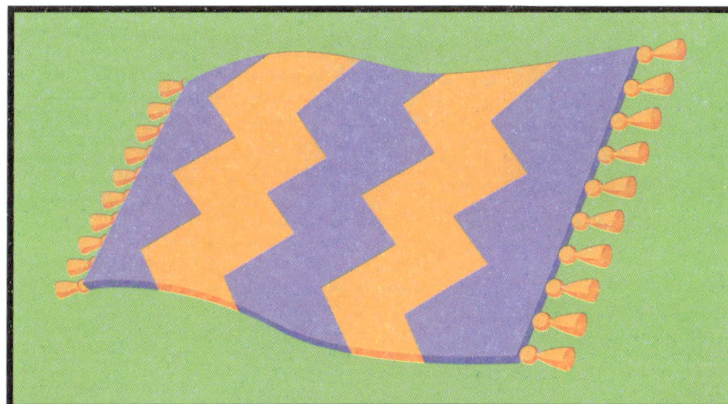

at	og	ug
c	fr	r
b	l	b
h	d	m

Got it! Not yet

Let's have some fun!

You need:

Draw a line from the  to the .

Got it! Not yet

I can draw a simple person.

You need:

Draw a face on the oval.

Got it! Not yet

I can draw a simple person.

You need:

Online Extra:
To go to this activity, use your smartphone camera, hover over this code, and click on the link. Or go to: **anywhereteacher.com/qr/14161/12**.

Draw a happy face.

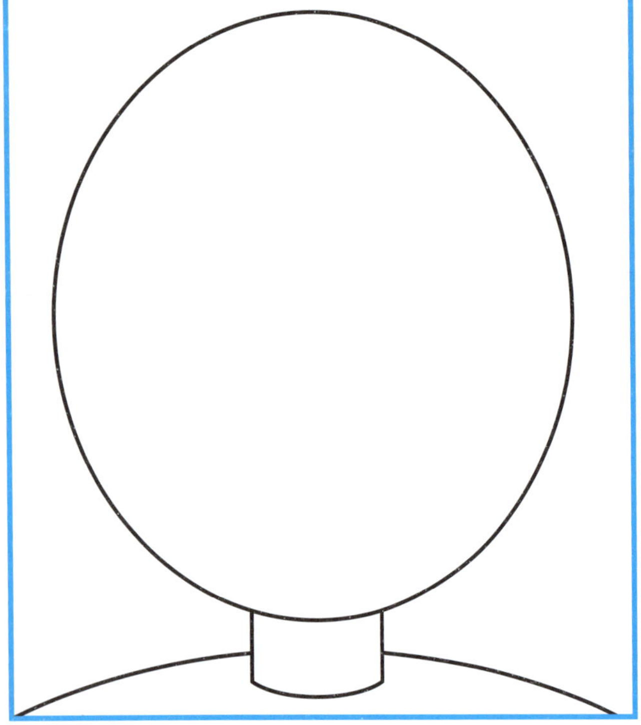

Draw a sad face.

Draw a scared face.

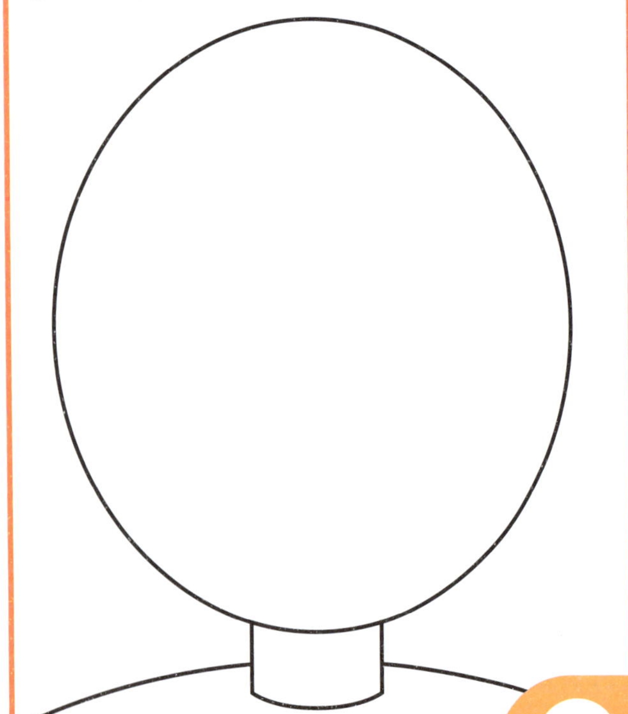

Draw a silly face.

Got it! Not yet

I can draw a simple person.

You need:

1 Draw a circle for the head.

2 Draw an oval for the body.

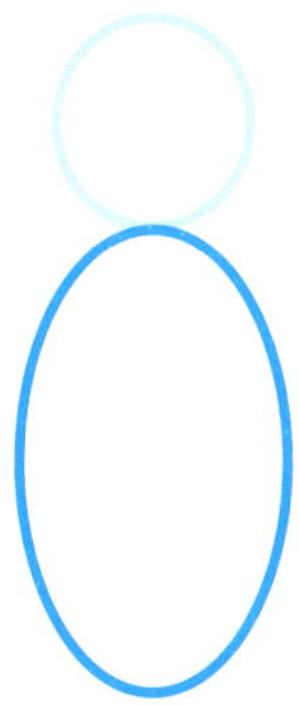

3 Draw lines for the arms and legs.

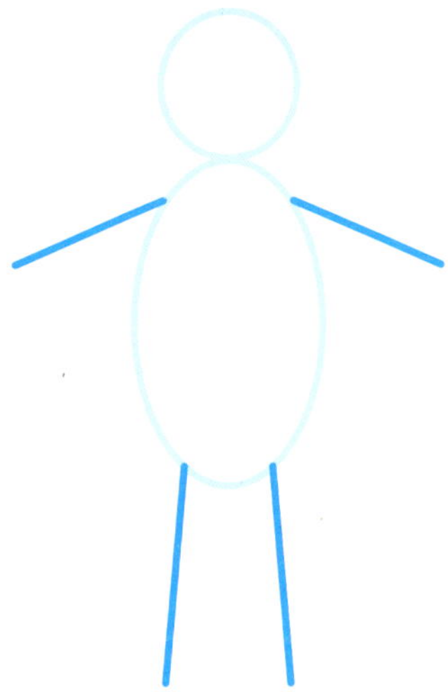

4 Draw circles for the hands and ovals for the feet.

Follow the steps to draw a person.

Got it! Not yet

I can draw a simple person.

You need:

Draw a picture of you and the clothes you are wearing right now.

Got it! Not yet

I can draw a simple person.

You need:

Draw a picture of your family.

Got it! Not yet

I can draw a simple person.

You need:

Draw a picture of you doing something you like to do.

Got it! Not yet

Let's have some fun!

You need:

Connect the dots from **A** to **Z**.
Color the picture.

Got it! Not yet

I can sort between letters and numbers.

Find the alphabet flash cards **Aa** and numbers flash cards 
.
Mix up all of the flash cards.
Sort the cards into the **letters** and **numbers** boxes below.

LETTERS

You need:

NUMBERS

Got it! Not yet

I can use stickers.

You need:

Find the stickers to complete the scene.

Got it! Not yet

I can use stickers.

You need:

Find the stickers to complete the scene.

Got it! Not yet

I can use stickers.

You need:

 Find the stickers to complete the scene.

Got it! Not yet

I can use stickers.

You need:

 Find the stickers to complete the scene.

Got it!

Not yet

Let's have some fun!

You need:

Circle what is different between **picture A** and **picture B**.

Picture A

Picture B

Got it! Not yet

Page 19

happy

sad

Page 27

excited

afraid

Page 57

embarrassed

proud

Page 85

mad

surprised

Page 113

disgusted

worried

Page 121

confused

silly

You need:

I can find my name in a group of words.

Use both sides of the paper to write your child's name as well as other names they may know. Make sure to use an uppercase letter for the first letter in each name. You may want to add your child's name more than once.

Cut out the names and mix them up, and then ask your child to find their name or another name.

Charlie

Got it! Not yet

Parent Tip:
Write their name on a blank piece of paper. Put the paper in the Write & Reuse™ sleeve and have your child practice writing their name.

Got it! Not yet

I can spell my name.

You need:

Use both sides of the paper to write the letters of your child's name as well as other names they may know. Make sure to use an uppercase letter for the first letter in each name.

Cut out the letters and mix them up. Then ask your child to find the letters of a name and put the letters in order to spell it out.

Got it! Not yet

Got it! Not yet

I can do my best to spell words.

You need:

Look at the picture.
Write the beginning letter to finish the word.

cat

dog

bus

hat

pig

jet

Got it! Not yet

I can do my best to spell words.

You need:

Look at the picture.
Write the beginning letter to finish the word.

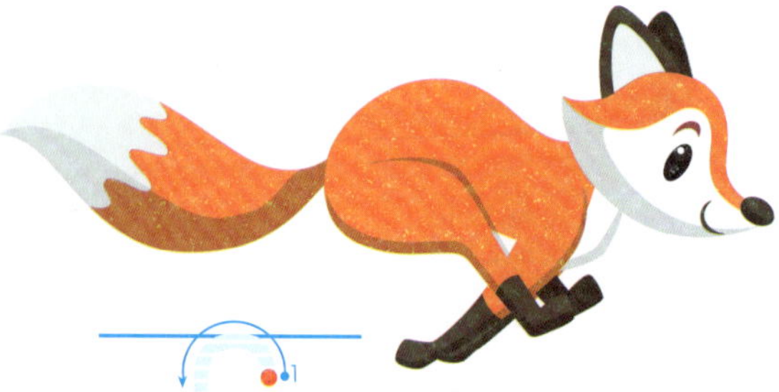

fox

bat

hen

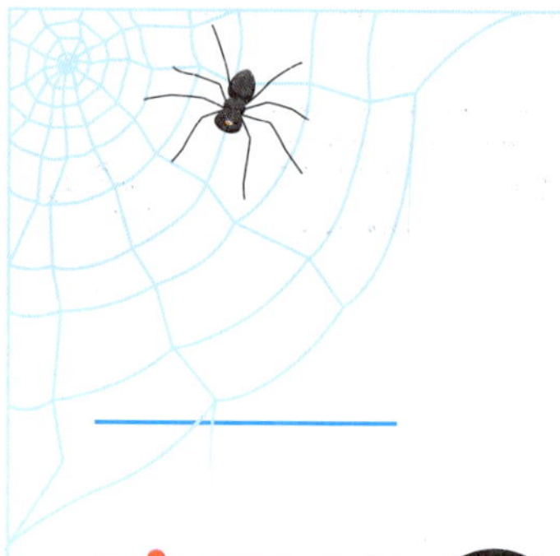

web

tub

pen

Got it! Not yet

I can do my best to spell words.

You need:

Look at the picture.
Write the beginning letter to finish the word.

ant

ill

jam

rat

ox

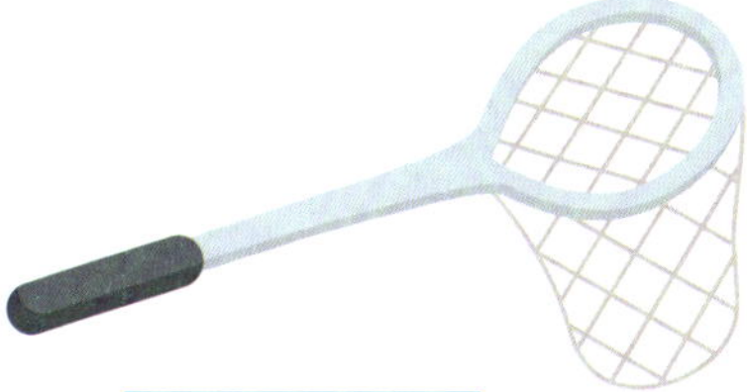

net

Got it! Not yet

I can do my best to spell words.

You need:

Look at the picture.
Write the beginning letter to finish the word.

log

egg

sun

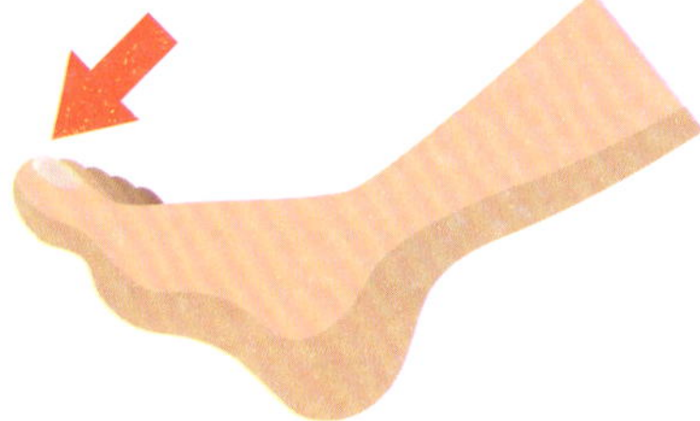

toe

yak

zoo

Got it! Not yet

I can do my best to spell words.

You need:

Look at the picture.
Write the beginning letter to finish the word.

van

ball

bell

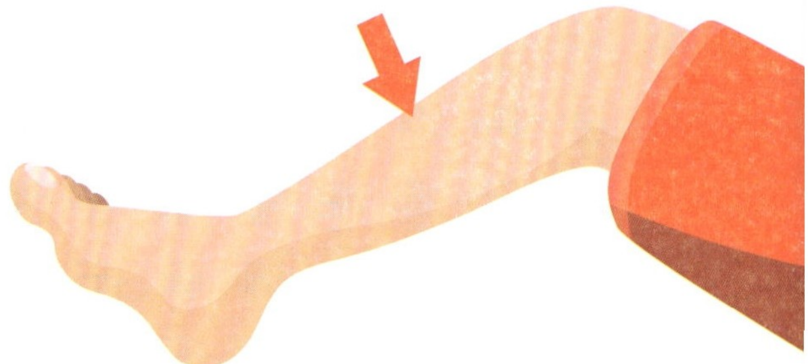

leg

corn

doll

Got it! Not yet

I can do my best to spell words.

Look at the picture.
Write the beginning letter to finish the word.

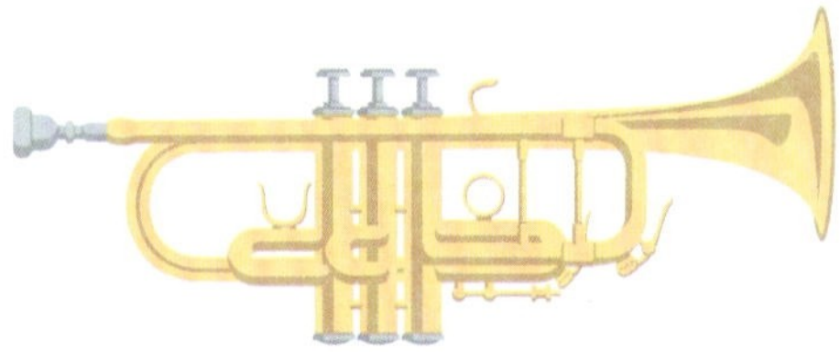

horn

nest

baby

duck

wood

ring

Got it! Not yet

Let's have some fun!

Connect the dots from **A** to **Z**.
Color the picture.

I can show that I understand that books are read from left to right and top to bottom.

You need:

Trace the lines from the ➡ on the left to the ● on the right.

Parent Tip:
Explain to your child readers read from the left to the right and from the top to the bottom.

Got it! Not yet

You need:

I can show that I understand that books are read from left to right and top to bottom.

Trace the line from ● to ●.
Start at the arrow ➡.

Online Extra:
To go to this activity, use your smartphone camera, hover over this code, and click on the link. Or go to: **anywhereteacher.com/qr/14161/13.**

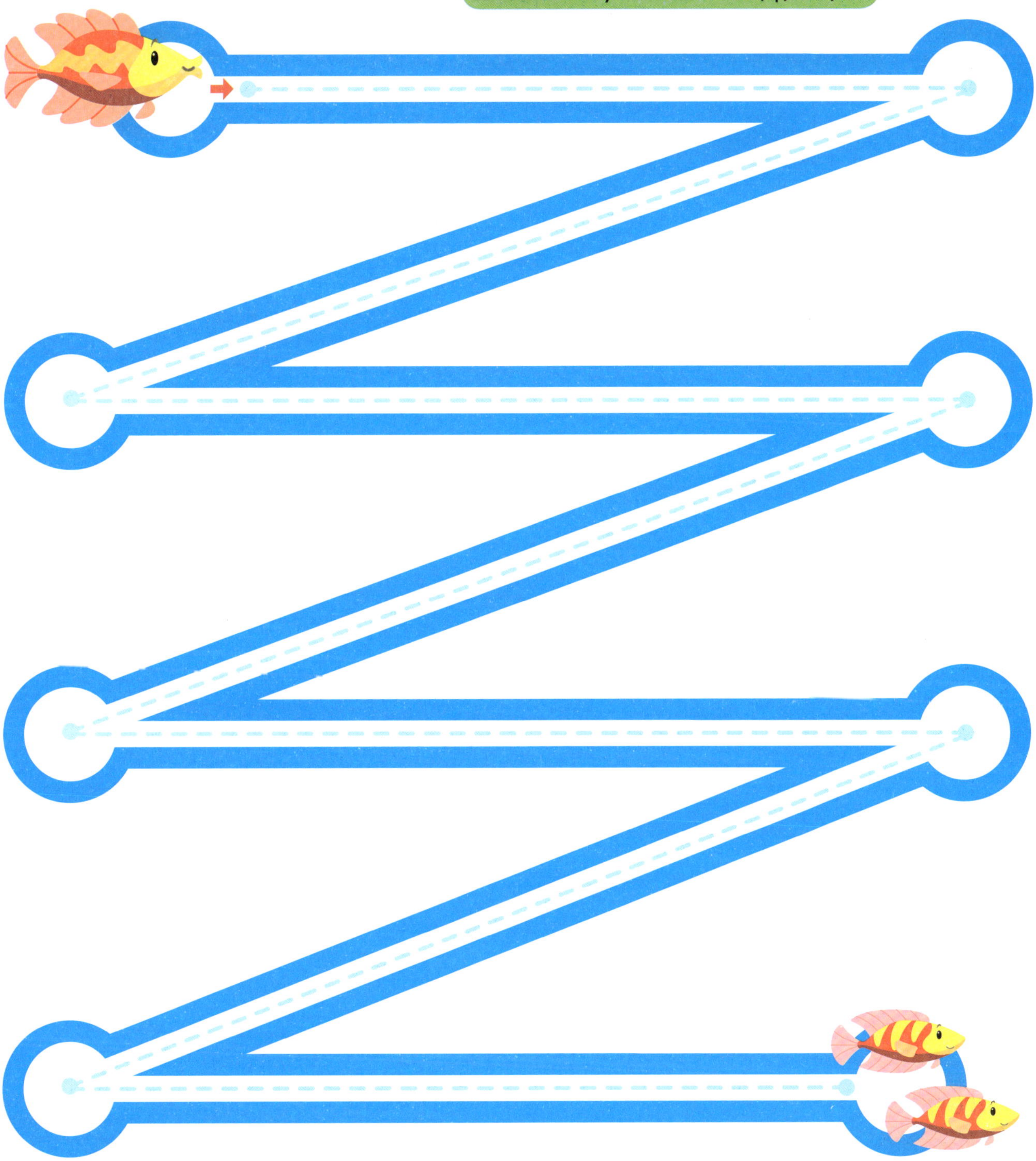

Got it! Not yet

You need:

I can show that I understand that books are read from left to right and top to bottom.

Trace the lines using the matching crayon color from the crayons on the left to the color words on the right.

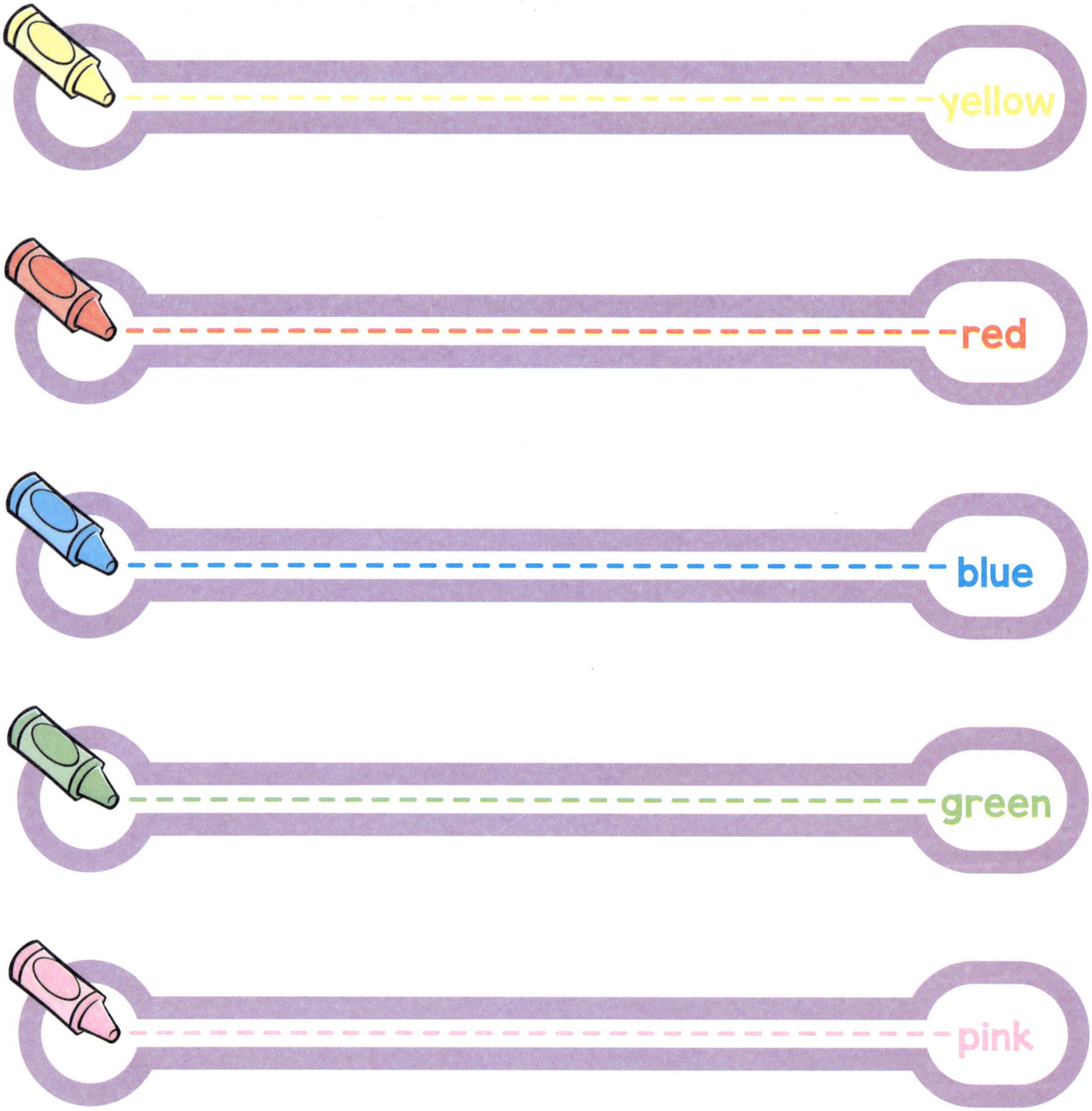

Parent Tip:
As you read with your child, move your finger from left to right and top to bottom to follow the words.

Got it!   Not yet

I can show that I understand that books are read from left to right and top to bottom.

You need:

Trace the line from ● to ●.
Start at the arrow ➡.

The red fish met

the yellow fish

by the crab.

Got it! Not yet

Let's have some fun!

You need:

Draw a line from the bear to the library.

Got it! Not yet

I can understand there are lots of different types of books.

You need:

Books come in all shapes and sizes.

✓ Put a check mark on the books you would like to read.

Parent Tip:
Have your child walk around your home and try to find five different things that can be read. It could be a newspaper, poetry, a nonfiction book, fiction book, or magazine.

Got it! Not yet

I can explore lots of different types of books.

You need:

This is **real**.

This is **make-believe**.

Circle the animals that look **real**.

Check the **make-believe** animals.

Got it! Not yet

Match the emotion.

You need:

Find and place the stickers to complete the scene.

Parent Tip:
Have your child tell a story about a time when they were happy.

Got it! Not yet

I can begin to understand direction words.

You need: 

in front

The rabbit is **in front** of the rock.

behind

The rabbit is **behind** the rock.

Circle the answer.

Which character is **in front** of ?  

Which character is **behind** ?  

Got it! Not yet

I can begin to understand position words.

You need:

up

Charlie is walking **up** the hill.

down

Jaz is walking **down** the hill.

Circle all of the swimming **up**.

Cross out all of the swimming **down**.

Got it! Not yet

You need:

I can begin to understand position words.

above

The butterfly is **above** the flower.

below

The butterfly is **below** the flower.

Circle the answer.

Which character is **below** ?

Which character is **above** ?

Got it! Not yet

I can begin to understand position words.

You need:

inside
A bird is sitting **inside** the nest.

outside
A bird is standing **outside** the nest.

Circle all of the birds **inside** a nest.
Cross out all of the birds **outside** a nest.

Got it! Not yet

I can begin to understand position words.

You need:

Circle who is **inside**.
Cross out who is **outside**.

Circle who is **up**.
Cross out who is **down**.

Circle who is **above**.
Cross out who is **below**.

Circle who is **in front**.
Cross out who is **behind**.

Got it! Not yet

I can begin to understand position words.

You need:

Circle the **middle**.

Circle the **top**.

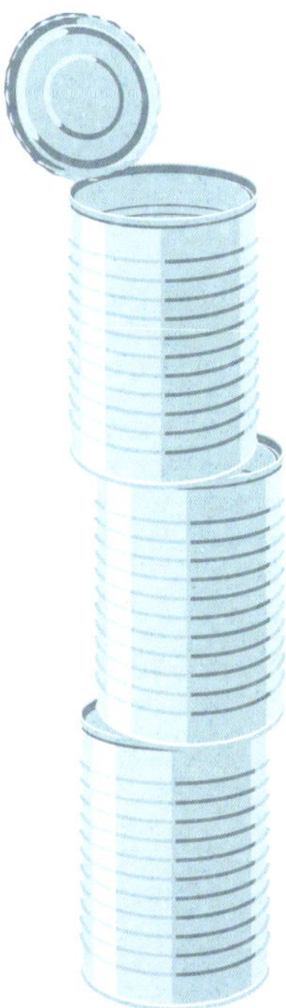

Circle the **middle**.

Circle the **bottom**.

Got it! Not yet

Let's have some fun!

You need:

Circle what is different between **picture A** and **picture B**.

Picture A

Picture B

Got it! Not yet

Match the emotion.

You need:

Find and place the stickers to complete the scene.

Parent Tip:
Have your child tell a story about a time when they were excited.

Got it!

Not yet

I can segment words into syllables.

You need:

dog	wagon	kangaroo

dog	*wa • gon*	*kan • ga • roo*

Clapping out the beats of the word allows you to count the syllables.

Online Extra: To go to this activity, use your smartphone camera, hover over this code, and click on the link. Or go to: **anywhereteacher.com/qr/14161/17.**

Say the name of each picture.

Clap and count the syllables.

Circle the number of syllables in each word.

Got it! Not yet

You need:

I can segment words into syllables.

Clap and count the syllables.

Circle the number of syllables in each word.

Got it! Not yet

I can segment words into syllables.

You need:

Use the cut-out squares from the next page.
Say the name of each picture out loud and count the number of syllables.
Sort the pieces into the correct boxes.

1 syllable

2 syllables

3 syllables

Got it! Not yet

I can segment words into syllables.

You need:

Cut out the squares below.
These will be used on the previous page.

Got it! Not yet

Parent Tip:
Use the alphabet press-out pieces as an additional sorting activity.

pi • an • o	ba • by	mouse	flow • er	piz • za
boat	en • vel • ope	rock • et	hat	rab • bit
book	cow	pan • da	bird	po • ta • to
ig • loo	cal • en • dar	air • plane	tree	ap • ple
bath • tub	key	to • ma • to	kite	clock

Got it! Not yet

Let's have some fun!

You need:

Connect the dots from **A** to **Z**.
Color the picture.

Got it! Not yet

You need:

I can tell someone what I like to read about.

The **title** of a book tells you what the book is about.

Read each title.

Circle the books you would like to read.

Parent Tip:
Visit AnywhereTeacher.com for more books!

Got it! Not yet

I can answer questions about a story I listened to.

You need:

Parents:
Please read the book **Charlie Digs** to your child.
Then ask the following questions.

Why did the author write this book?

To teach about frogs.

To tell a funny story about a dog, Charlie.

What does Charlie like to do?

sleep

dig

Where does Charlie dig?

under the log

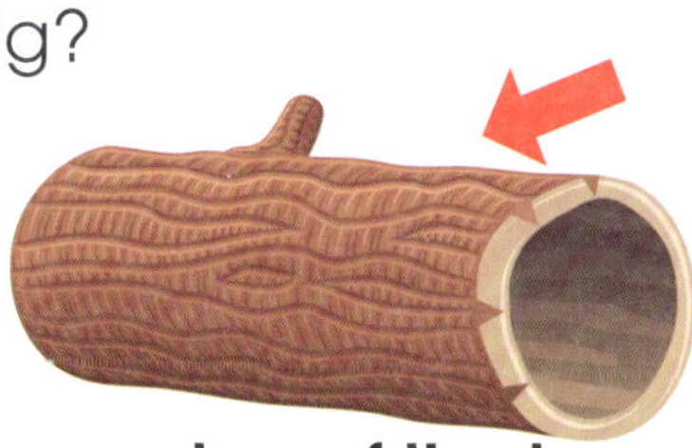

on top of the log

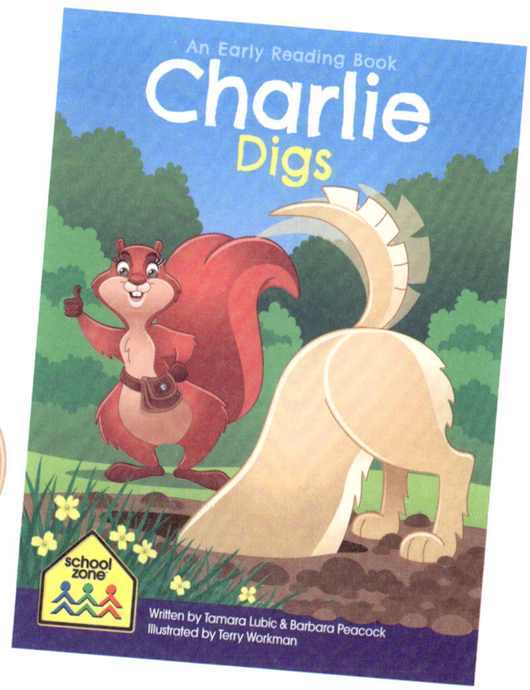

In the end, what did Charlie find?

a food bowl

an acorn

Do you like reading the book *Charlie Digs*?

Yes

No

Parent Tip:
Go to your local library and read 3 books by the same author. Try Eric Carle, Matt de la Peña, Anna Dewdney, Vashti Harrison, Kevin Henkes, Ezra Jack Keats, Erik Litwin, Anna McQuinn, Juana Medina, Robert Munsch, Laura Numeroff, Kenard Pak, and Mo Willems.

Got it! Not yet

Let's have some fun!

You need:

Color the scene.

1 =  2 =  3 =  4 =  5 = 

Got it! Not yet

I can tell a story in order.

You need:

Cut out the story panels on the right.
Paste the story panels in order on the boxes on the left.

1

2

3

Got it! Not yet

Let's have some fun!

You need:

Circle all of the .

Got it! Not yet

You need:

I can show that I understand that objects around me can be measured.

Circle how many ☐ long each measures.

3 4 5

1 2 3

1 2 3

3 4 5

Got it! Not yet

You need: 

I can show that I understand that objects around me can be measured.

Circle how many ☐ long each lily pad measures.

3 4 5

1	2	3	4	5	6	7

1 2 3

1	2	3	4	5	6	7

3 4 5

1	2	3	4	5	6	7

1 2 3

1	2	3	4	5	6	7

Got it! Not yet

I can show that I understand that objects around me can be measured.

You need:

Circle how many ☐ long each caterpillar measures.

Online Extra:
To go to this activity, use your smartphone camera, hover over this code, and click on the link. Or go to: **anywhereteacher.com/qr/14161/14**.

1 2 3

1	2	3	4	5	6	7

3 4 5

1	2	3	4	5	6	7

1 2 3

1	2	3	4	5	6	7

4 5 6

1	2	3	4	5	6	7

Got it! Not yet

You need:

I can show that I understand that objects around me can be measured.

Circle how many ☐ tall each tree measures.

5 6 7 3 4 5 6 7 8

Got it! Not yet

I can show that I understand that objects around me can be measured.

Circle how many ☐ tall each measures.

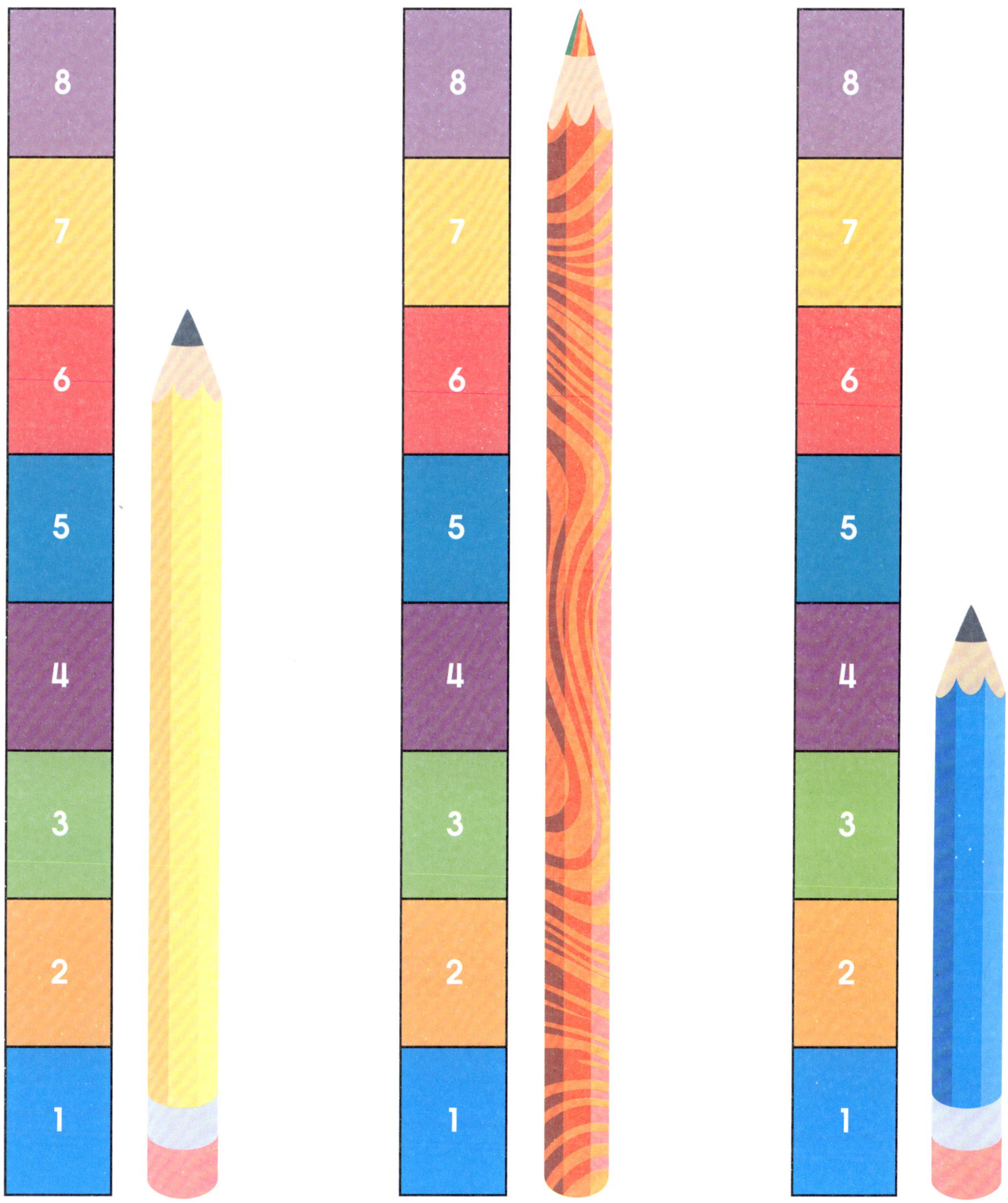

5 6 7 | 6 7 8 | 3 4 5

Got it! Not yet

You need:

I can use the words long, longer, short, and shorter when I measure objects.

shorter longer

Draw a pencil that is **shorter**.

Draw a snake that is **longer**.

Got it! Not yet

You need:

I can answer questions about what I read.

Parents:
Please read the book **What Grows on Trees?** to your child.
Then ask the following questions.

Why did the author write this book?

To tell us what grows on trees.

To tell us about hamburgers.

Do oranges grow on trees?

Do rabbits grow on trees?

How does this book make you feel?

Silly

Sad

Did you like reading *What Grows on Trees?*

Got it! Not yet

I can use the words **big**, **biggest**, **small**, and **smallest** when I measure objects.

You need:

smallest

biggest

Look at the pictures in each row.

✓ Check the picture that is the **smallest.**

✗ Cross out the picture that is the **biggest**.

Got it! Not yet

You need:

I can use the words tall, tallest, short, and shortest when I measure objects.

shortest tallest

Look at the pictures in each row.

✓ Check the picture that is the **shortest**.

✗ Cross out the picture that is the **tallest**.

Got it! Not yet

You need:

I can use the words long, longer, short, and shorter when I measure objects.

Color the **shorter** snake  orange.

Color the **longer** snake  blue.

Got it! Not yet

You need:

I can use the words tall, tallest, short, and shortest when I measure objects.

Color the **tallest** flowers pink.

Color the **shortest** flowers yellow.

Got it! Not yet

I can use the words big, biggest, small, and smallest when I measure objects.

You need:

Draw a line from the big animals to **BIG**.
Draw a line from the small animals to **small**.

BIG small

Got it! Not yet

Let's have some fun!

You need:

Draw a line from the  to the .

Got it! Not yet

I can answer questions about what I read.

You need:

Parents:
Please read the book **The Good Bad Cat** to your child. Then ask the following questions.

Why did the author write this book?

To tell a story about a cat chasing a mouse.

To teach you how to feed a cat.

When the cat made a mess, what did they tell the cat?

Good Cat

Bad Cat

What was the cat chasing?

 **A bird**

 **A mouse**

At the end, why did they tell the cat "Good cat"?

The cat chased the mouse out the door.

The cat cleaned up the mess he made.

Did you like reading *The Good Bad Cat*?

 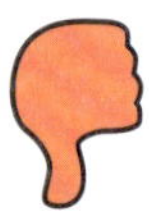

Got it! Not yet

You need:

I can predict what might happen next in a story.

Look at the first picture in each row.
Circle the picture that shows what will happen **next**.

Parent Tip:
Go to your local library and let your child check out a book. While reading to your child, be sure to stop along the way and give them an opportunity to predict what might happen next.

Got it!   Not yet

You need:

I can predict what might happen next in a story.

Look at the first picture in each row.

Circle the picture that shows what will happen **next**.

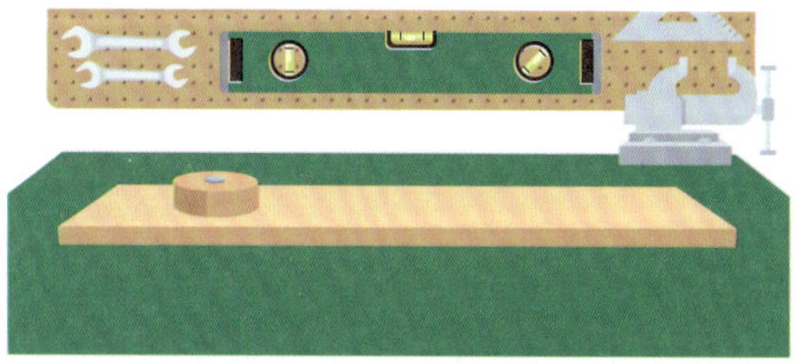

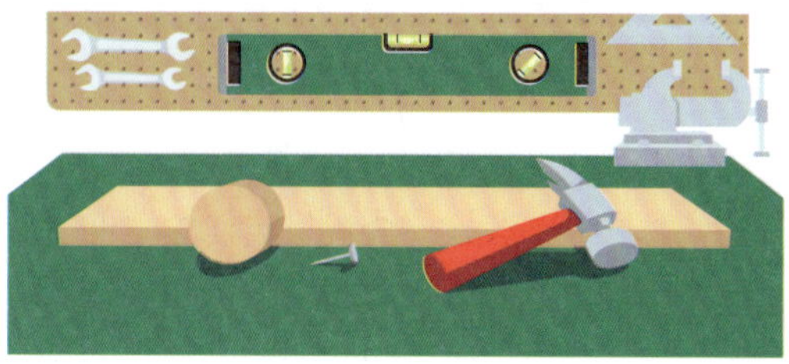

Got it! Not yet

You need:

I can predict what might happen next in a story.

Look at the pictures in each row.
Circle the picture that shows what will happen **next**.

Got it! Not yet

Let's have some fun!

Circle what is different between **picture A** and **picture B**.

Picture A

Picture B

Got it! Not yet

Match the emotion.

You need:

Find and place the stickers to complete the scene.

Parent Tip:
Have your child tell a story about a time when they were embarrassed.

Got it! Not yet

I can predict what might happen next in a story.

Look at the pictures in each row.
Circle the picture that shows what will happen **next**.

Got it! Not yet

You need:

I can show that I understand that objects around me can be measured.

Circle how long each object measures.

1 2 3

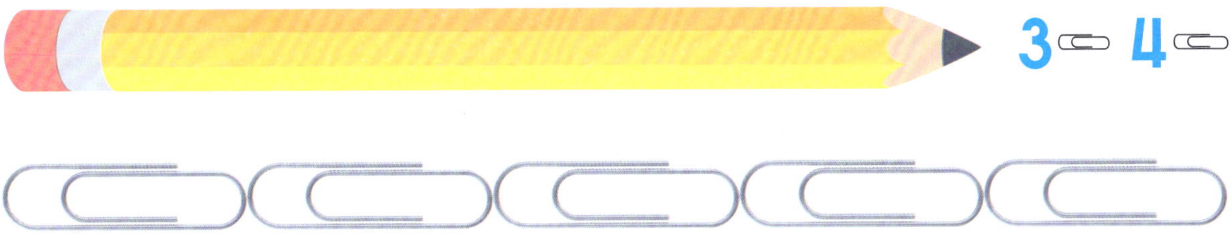

3 4 5

4 5 6

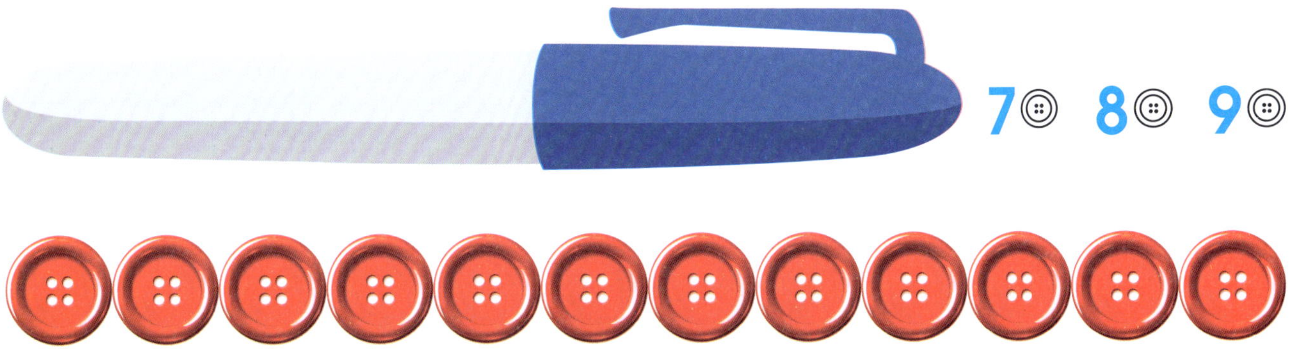

7 8 9

Got it! Not yet

You need:

I can show that I understand that objects around me can be measured.

Circle how long each object measures.

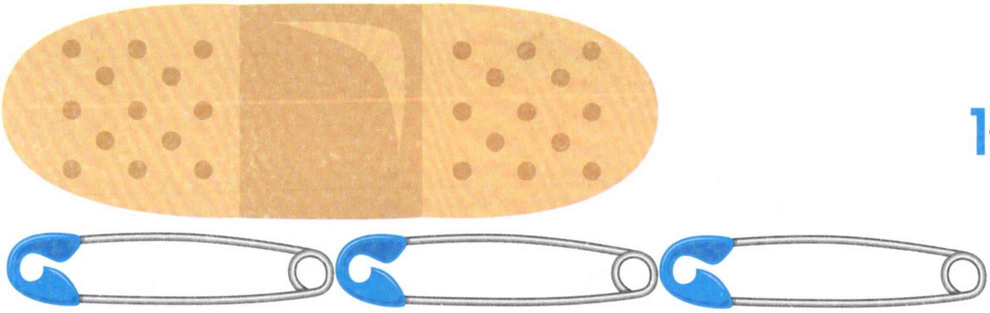

1 2 3

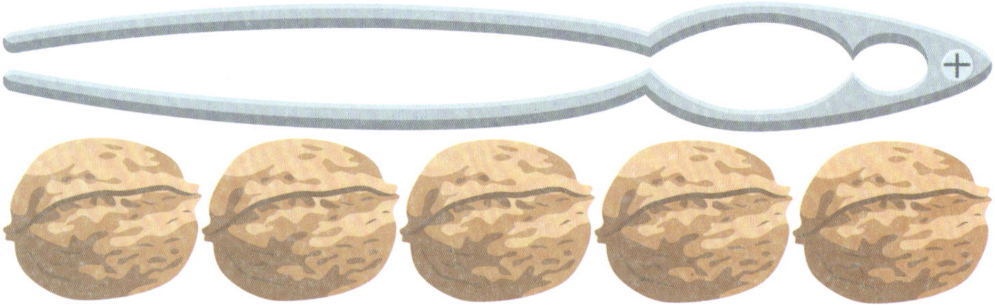

3 4 5

2 3 4

2 3 4

Got it! Not yet

You need:

I can show that I understand that objects around me can be measured.

Circle how long each object measures.

3 4 5

4 5 6

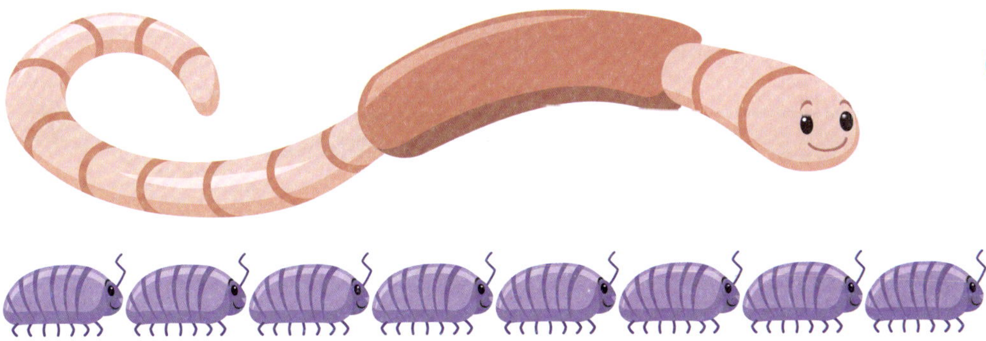

6 7 8

5 6 7

Got it! Not yet

Let's have some fun!

You need:

Connect the dots from **A** to **Z**.
Color the picture.

Got it! Not yet

You need:

I can show that I understand that objects around me can be measured.

Circle how many tall each object measures.

5 6 7

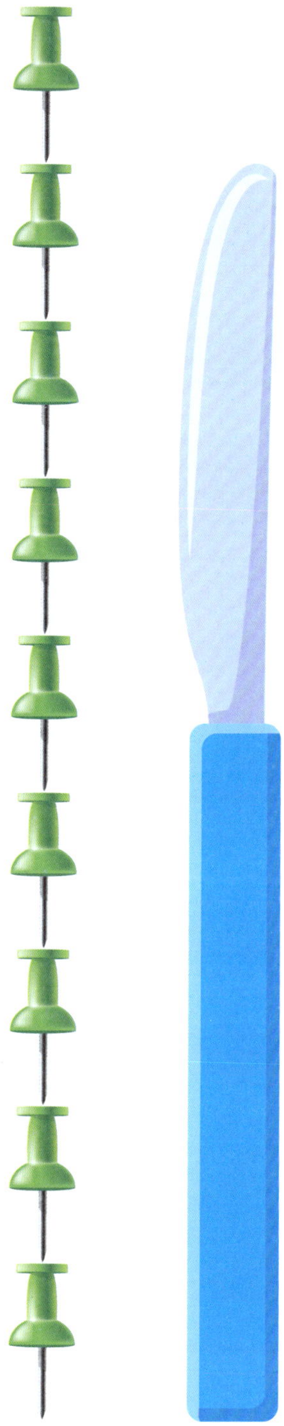

6 7 8

5 6 7

Got it! Not yet

You need:

I can show that I understand that objects around me can be measured.

Circle how many tall each object measures.

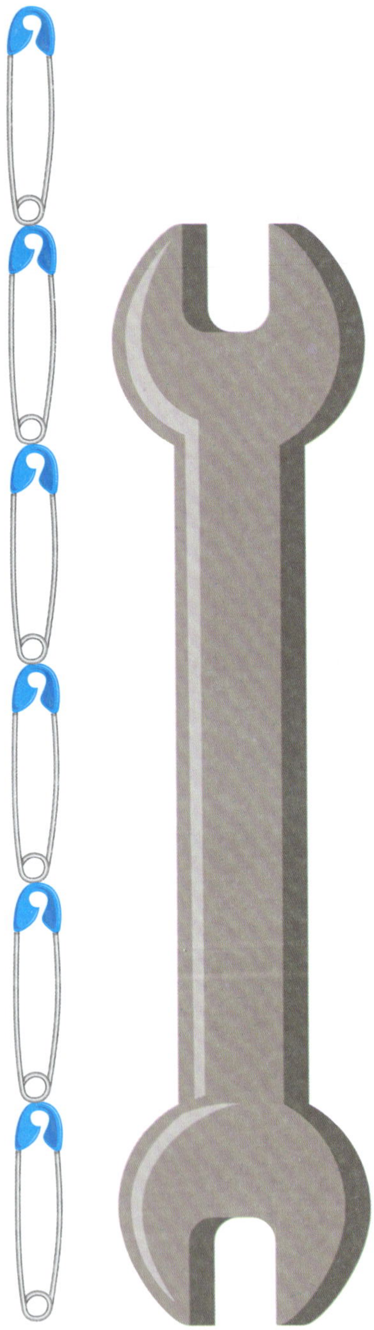

5 6 7

2 3 4

3 4 5

Got it! Not yet

You need:

I can show that I understand that objects around me can be measured.

Circle how many tall each object measures.

4 5 6

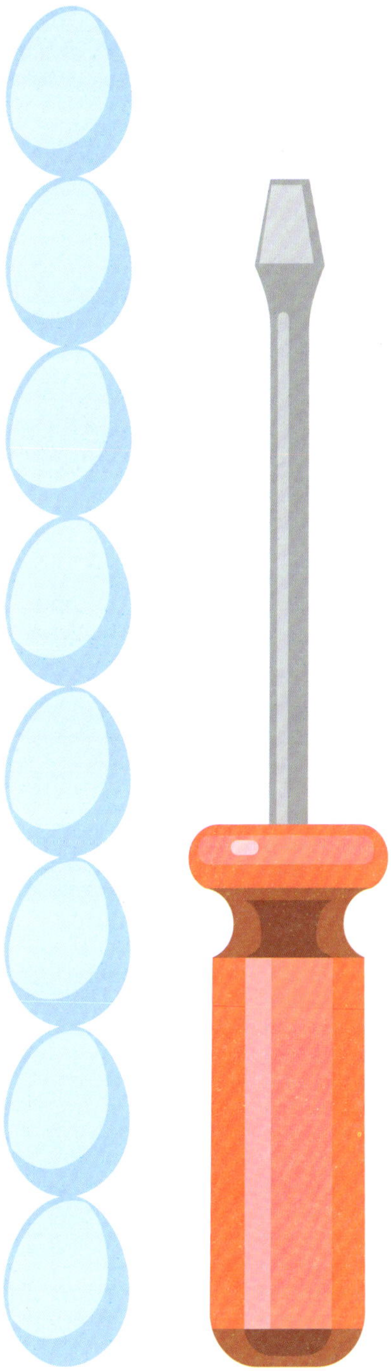

6 7 8

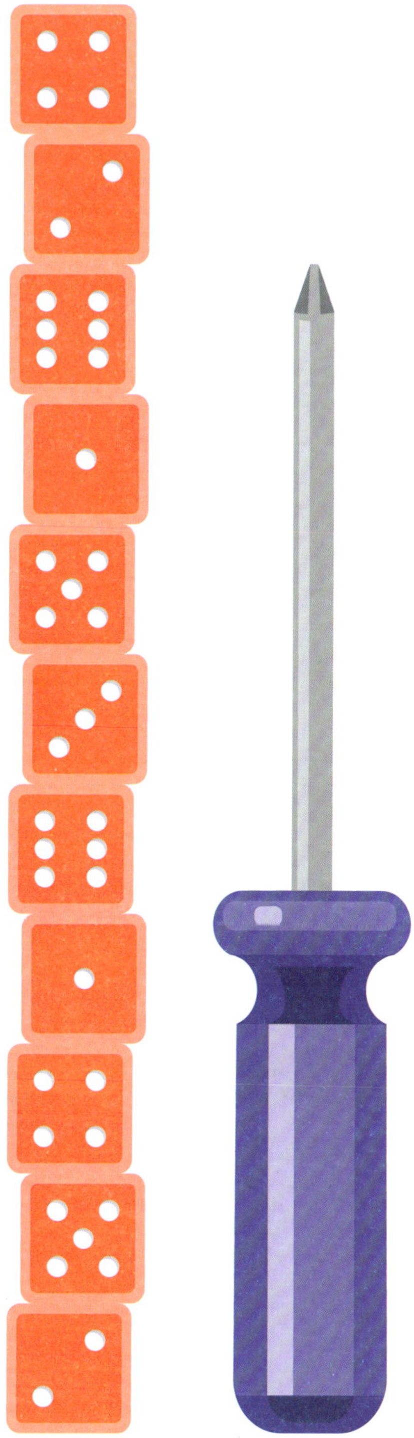

7 8 9

Got it! Not yet

Let's have some fun!

You need:

Circle all of the .

Got it! Not yet

You need:

I can sort groups of objects.

Draw a line from each item to the correct basket.

Got it! Not yet

I can sort groups of objects.

You need:

Draw a line from each item to the correct plate.

Got it! Not yet

I can create new shapes or designs using other shapes.

You need: scissors

Cut out the shapes on this page to use on pages 71-73.
Use these cutouts to make the shapes on the next pages.

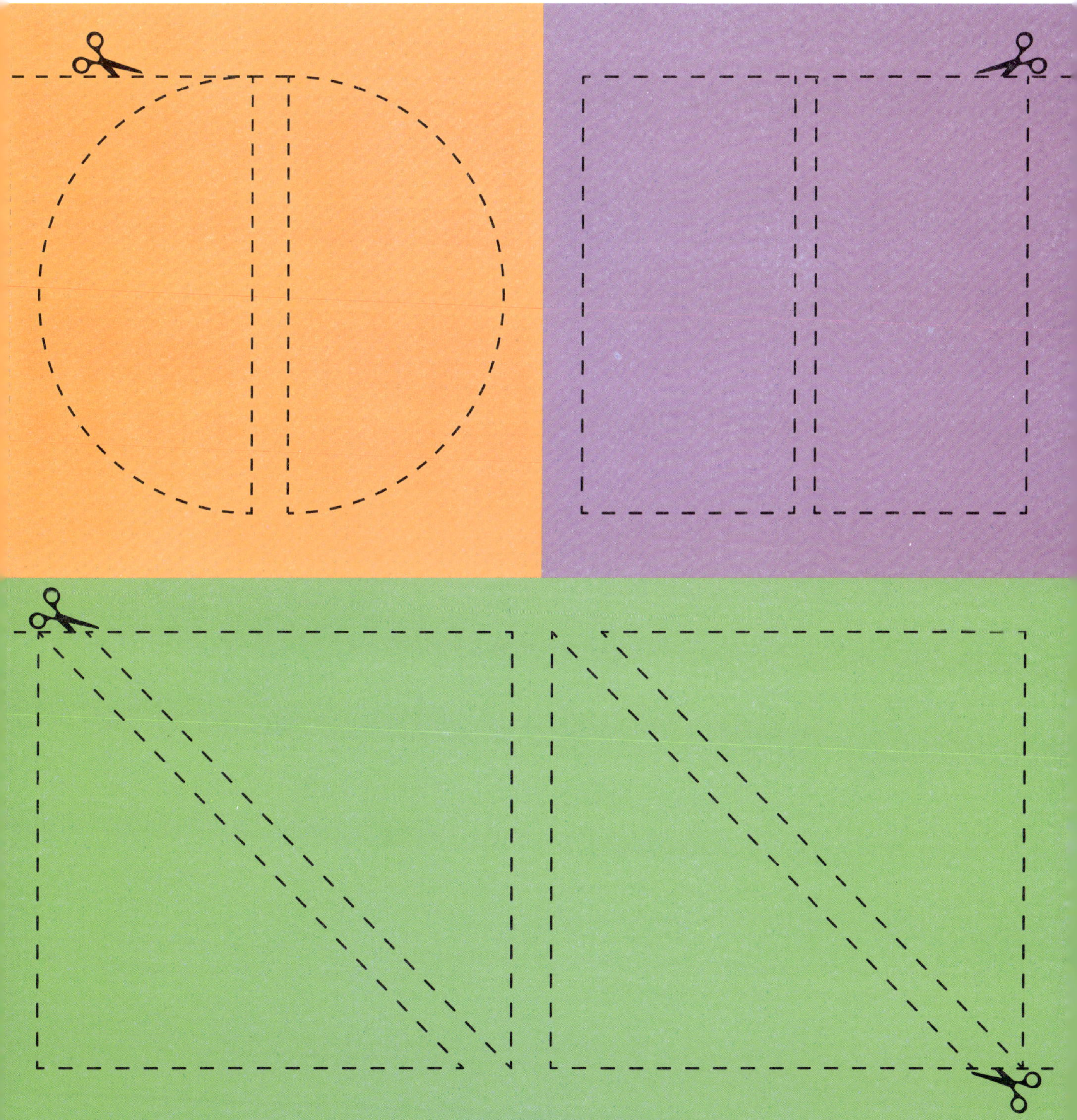

Got it! Not yet

You need:

I can create new shapes or designs using other shapes.

Use the cutouts to make the shapes on the page.
Do NOT glue them down.

Got it! Not yet

You need:

I can create new shapes or designs using other shapes.

Use the cutouts to make the shapes on the page.
Do NOT glue them down.

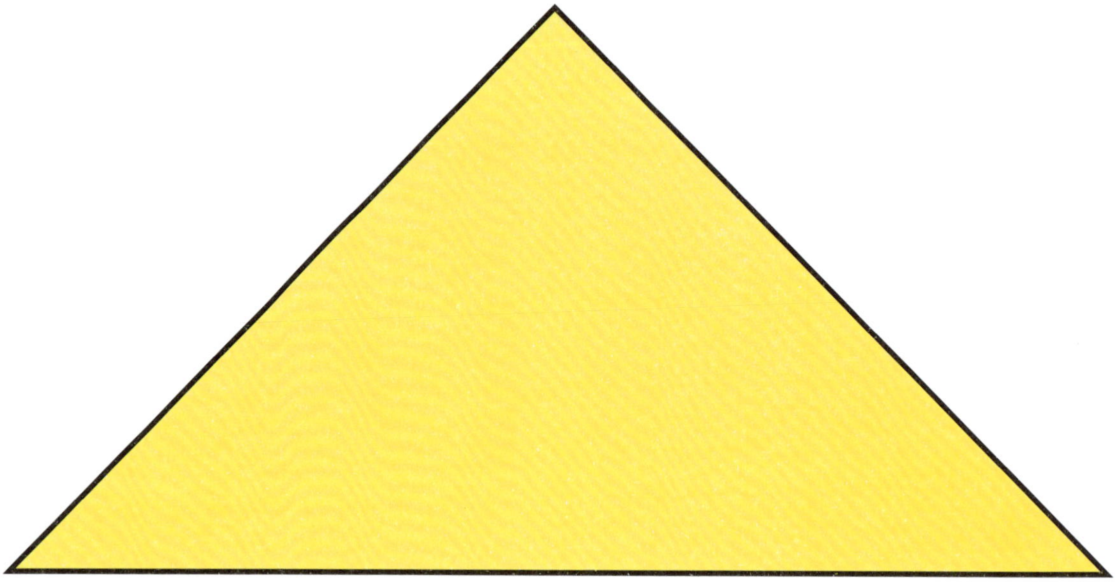

Got it! Not yet

I can create new shapes or designs using other shapes.

You need:

Use the cutouts to make the shapes on the page.
Do NOT glue them down.

Got it! Not yet

You need:

Let's have some fun!

Draw a line from the  to the .

Got it! Not yet

I can answer questions about a story I listened to.

Parents:
Please read the book **Big Cats** to your child.
Then ask the following questions.

Why did the author write this book?

To teach us about frogs.

To teach us about big cats.

What do tigers have?

stripes

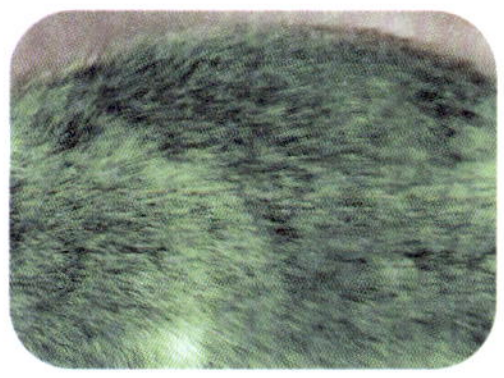

green fur

What do tigers, lions, and jaguars do?

squeak

ROAR!

What do lions live in with their families?

pride

house

What animal would you like to read more about?

lion

jaguar

tiger

snow leopard

Got it! Not yet

You need:

I can explain what I learned from an informational text.

Circle the answer.

What is the thick fur around a male lion's neck called?

A scarf **A mane** **A coat**

Draw and color what is missing on the male lion.

Got it! Not yet

I can explain what I learned from an informational text.

You need:

Circle the answer.

What color are the stripes on a tiger?

red black blue

Draw and color the stripes on the tiger.

Got it! Not yet

I can explain what I learned from an informational text.

You need:

Circle the answer.

What are the flower-shaped spots on a jaguar called?

tulips **lilies** **rosettes**

Draw and color the missing spots on the jaguar.

Got it! Not yet

I can begin to understand that there are tools to measure.

You need:

A **ruler** helps you measure how **long** something is.
To measure something you place the end of the object you want to measure at **zero**. The number on the ruler tells you how long the object is.

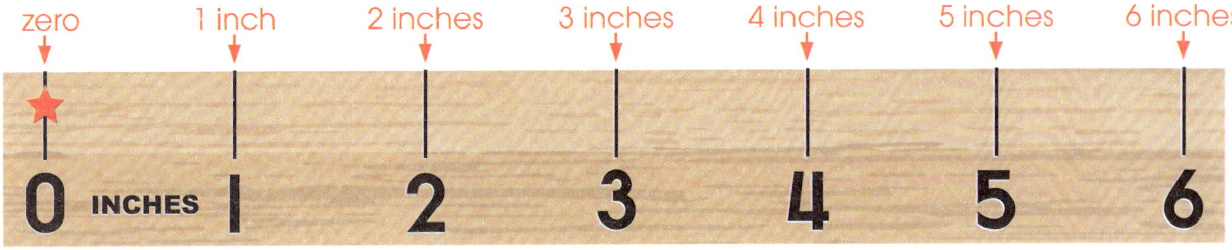

Cut out the ruler and use it to measure the objects.
Write how **long** each object is.

Got it! Not yet

I can begin to understand that there are tools to measure.

You need:

Parent Tip:
Measure other things around the house using this ruler.

Use the cut-out ruler to measure the objects. Write how tall each object is.

Got it! Not yet

Let's have some fun!

You need: 

 Circle all of the .

Got it! Not yet

I can begin to understand that there are tools to measure.

You need:

Use the cut-out ruler to measure the objects.
Write how long each object is.

Got it! Not yet

You need:

I can begin to understand that there are tools to measure.

Use the cut-out ruler to measure the objects.
Write how tall each object is.

Got it! Not yet

I can talk about my favorite author or book.

You need:

Circle the answer.

Which of these four books is your favorite?

Draw the cover of your favorite book.
Write the author's name.

Parent Tip:
After reading to your child, allow them to retell one of their favorites to you.

Got it! Not yet

Match the emotion.

You need:

Find and place the stickers to complete the scene.

I can say what's the same and different about two stories.

Read these two picture stories.

Fire Station Fun

Zoo Trip

Got it! Not yet

You need:

Compare the two picture stories.

✓ Put a check mark in each column if it appears in the story.

The first one is done for you.

	Both	Fire Station Fun	Zoo Trip
	✓		

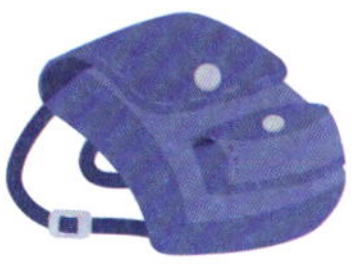			

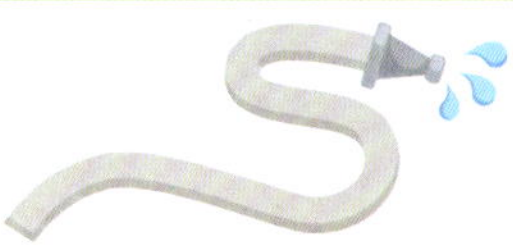			

Got it! Not yet

Let's have some fun!

You need:

Color the scene.

1 = 2 = 3 = 4 = 5 =

6 = 7 =

Got it! Not yet

You need:

I can begin to understand that there are tools to measure how heavy or light an object is.

A **scale** is used to measure weight. When two objects are put on a balance scale, the heavier object will drop down and the lighter object will lift up.

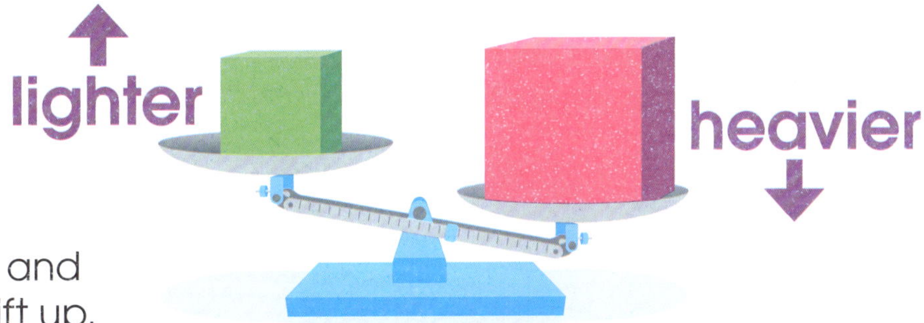

Balance Scale

Circle the animal that is **heavier**.

Circle the animal that is **lighter**.

Online Extra:
To go to this activity, use your smartphone camera, hover over this code, and click on the link. Or go to: anywhereteacher.com/qr/14161/15.

Got it! Not yet

You need:

I can begin to understand that there are tools to measure how heavy or light an object is.

Circle the object that is **heavier**.
The first one is done for you.

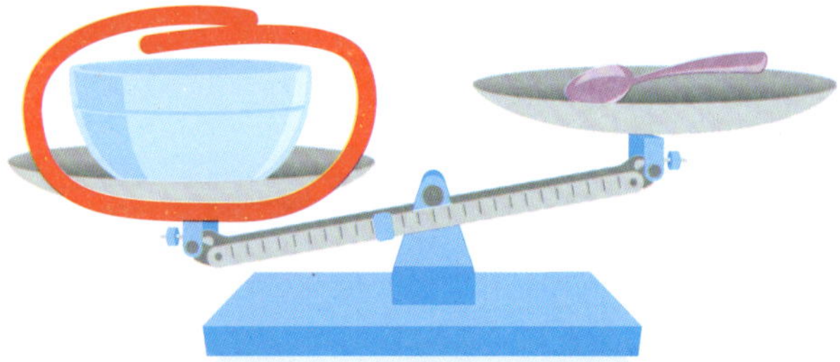

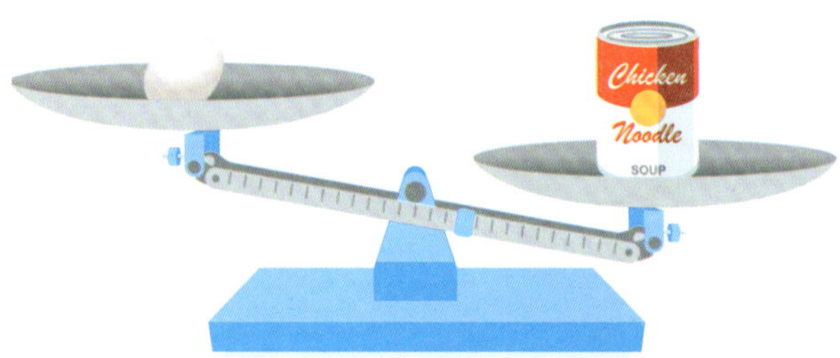

Got it! Not yet

You need:

I can begin to understand that there are tools to measure how heavy or light an object is.

Circle the object that is **lighter**.
The first one is done for you.

Got it! Not yet

You need:

I can begin to understand how heavy or light an object is.

Circle all of the objects that are **heavier** than an apple.

Circle all of the objects that are **lighter** than an apple.

Got it! Not yet

Let's have some fun!

You need:

Connect the dots from **A** to **Z**.
Color the picture.

Got it! Not yet

I can begin to understand weight.

You need:

Oba the bear weighs the **most** because he weighs more than Levi the beaver and Nestor the mouse.

weighs **less** weighs **more** weighs **most**

Look at the pictures in each row.

✓ Check the picture that weighs the **most** in each row.

Got it! Not yet

I can begin to understand weight.

You need:

Autumn the squirrel weighs the **most** because she weighs more than a pine cone and an acorn.

Look at the pictures in each row.

✓ Check the picture that weighs the **most** in each row.

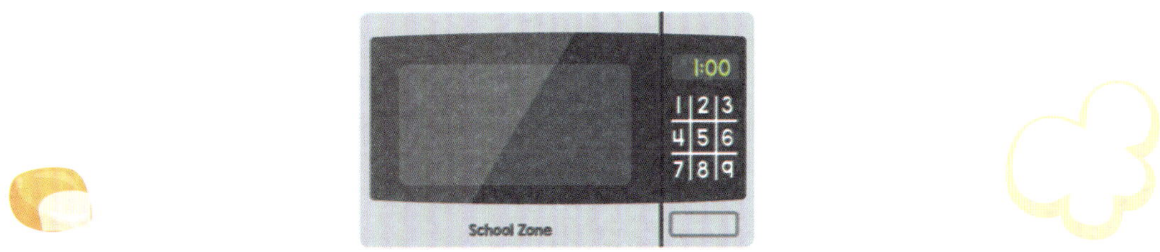

Got it! Not yet

You need:

I can understand the different reasons why people write. (make lists, tell stories, teach others, etc.)

We write things for different reasons.
Draw a line to where you would find these types of writing.
The first one is done for you.

This is a **grocery list**. We make grocery lists to remember what we need from a store.

This is a **recipe card**. We use recipe cards to tell us how food needs to be cooked.

This is a **letter**. We write letters to tell other people something when we cannot see them in person.

This is a **book**. We write books to share longer stories or large amounts of information with more than one person.

Parent Tip:
Write a letter with your child to another member of your family.

Got it! Not yet

Online Extra:
To go to this activity, use your smartphone camera, hover over this code, and click on the link. Or go to: **anywhereteacher.com/qr/14161/16.**

I can understand the different reasons why people write.

(make lists, tell stories, teach others, etc.)

You need:

a book

a letter

a recipe

a list

Circle the answer.

If you were going to the store and you don't want to forget anything you need, you would want to write:

If you had a long story you wanted to share with the whole world, you would want to write:

If you wanted to share how to cook something, you would want to write:

If you wanted to share a fun story with your grandparents, you would want to write:

Parent Tip:
Have your child help you the next time you make a shopping list.

Got it! Not yet

I can label my pictures.

Cut the labels from the page.
Paste them in the scene to label the things in the picture.

You need:

sun

bird

cat

kid

tree

pond

Got it! Not yet

I can write other words that are important to me. (mom, dad, siblings' names, etc.)

Draw a picture of your family.
Label everyone in the picture.

Let's have some fun!

You need:

Draw a line from the  to the .

Got it! Not yet

I can begin to understand graphs.

You need:

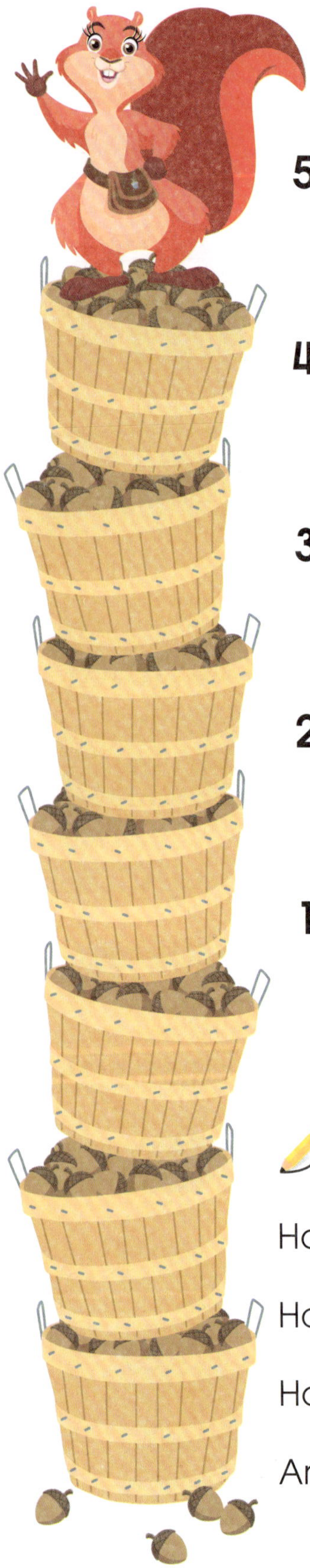

Use the graph to answer the questions.
Circle your answer.

How many acorns are there? 3 4 5

How many nests are there? 1 2 3

How many birds are there? 3 4 5

Are there more birds than acorns? yes no

Got it! Not yet

I can begin to understand graphs.

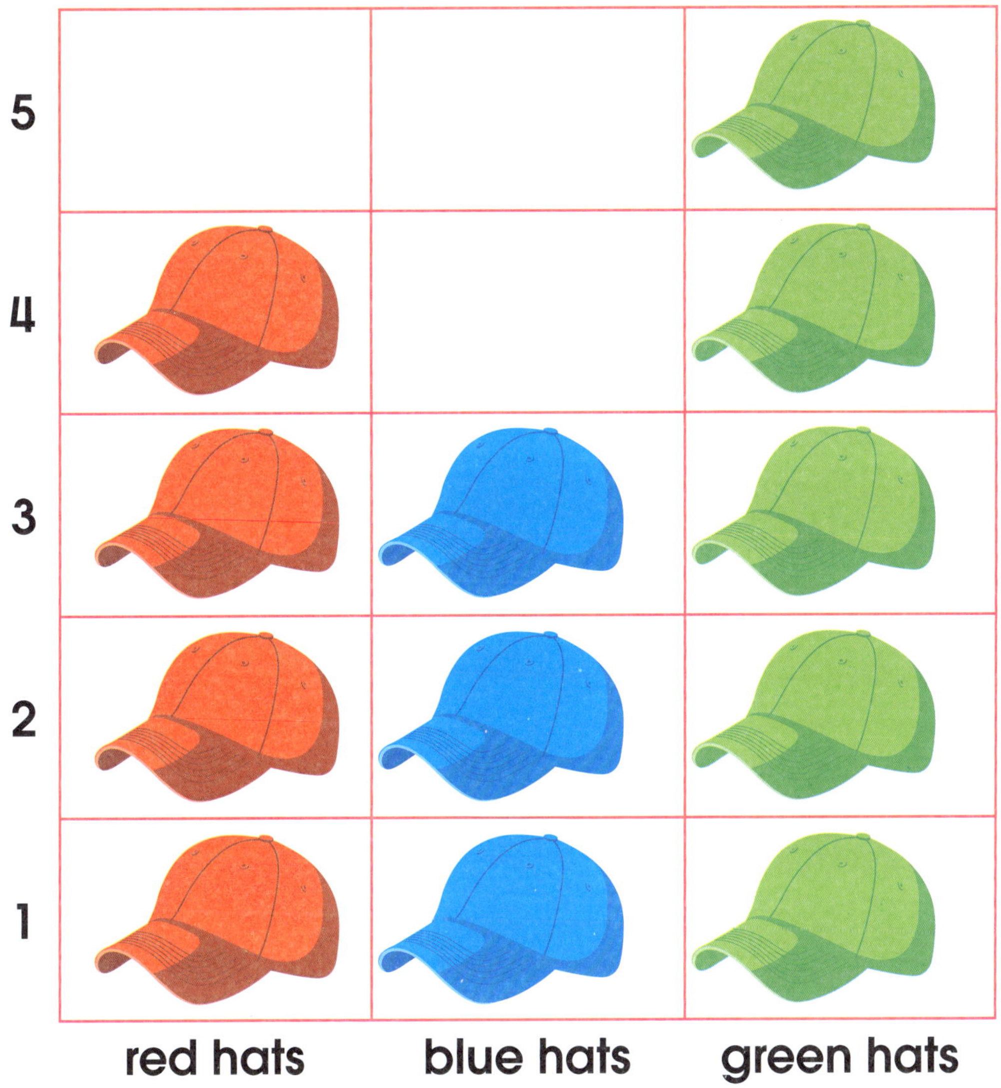

Use the graph to answer the questions.

Circle your answer.

How many blue hats are there? **3 4 5**

How many green hats are there? **3 4 5**

How many red hats are there? **3 4 5**

Are there more green hats than red hats? **yes no**

Got it! Not yet

I can use pictures and words to write.

You need:

Draw a picture to tell a story about a time when you were happy.
Label your picture.
Share your story with a family member.

Parent Tip:
Have your child practice this over and over on other pieces of paper.

Got it! Not yet

I can add one more in my head (up to 10).

You need:

2 and **one more** is **3**.

Circle the hand that shows **one more** than the first one in each row.

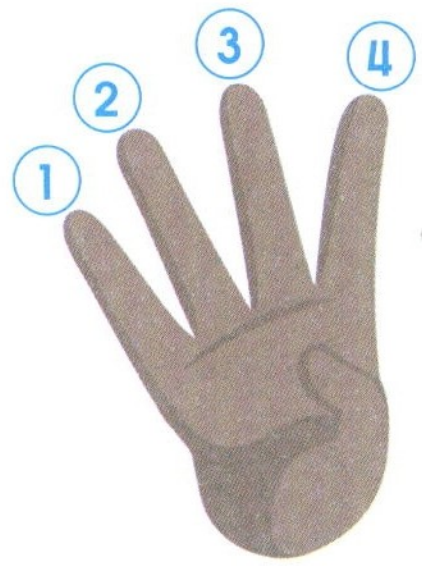

Got it!

Not yet

I can add one more in my head (up to 10).

Circle the number that comes next.

10 9

6 8

8 5

Got it! Not yet

I can use pictures and words to write.

You need:

Would you rather play in the day or at night ?
Draw a picture of you playing.
Add labels to your picture.
Share your story with a family member.

Got it! Not yet

I can join or combine a group of objects.

How many are there **in all**?
Write the number.
The first one is done for you.

Parent Tip:
If this is easy for your child, repeat these activities with objects such as pennies with answers up to 10.

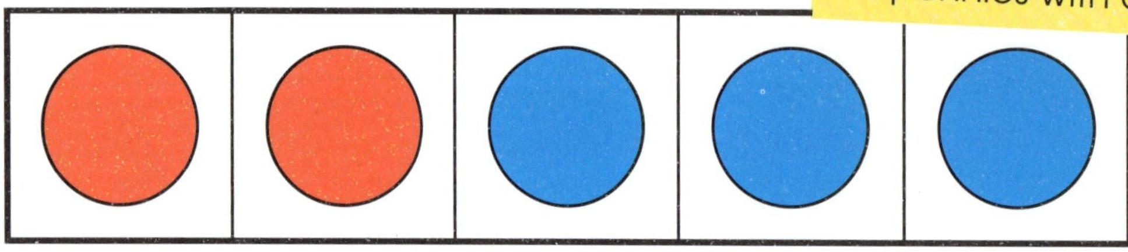

2 + 3 = 5

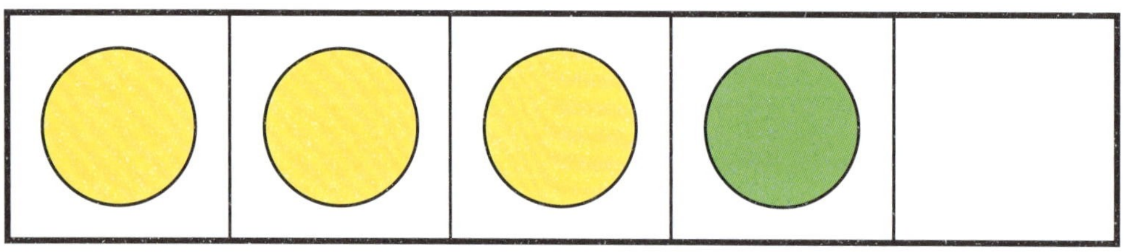

3 + 1 = ____

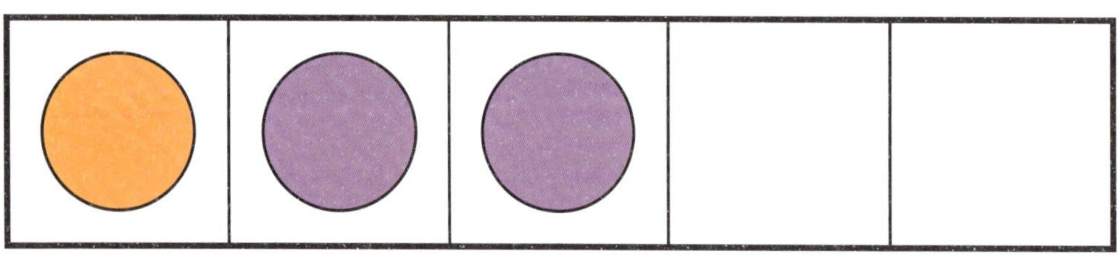

1 + 2 = ____

Got it! Not yet

I can join or combine a group of objects.

How many are there **in all**? Write the number.

1 + 1 = ____

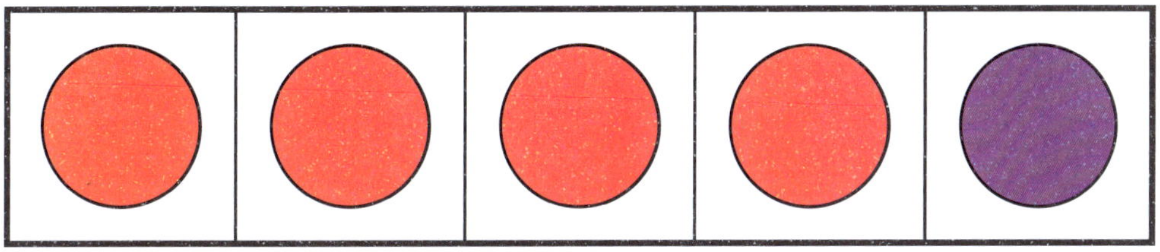

4 + 1 = ____

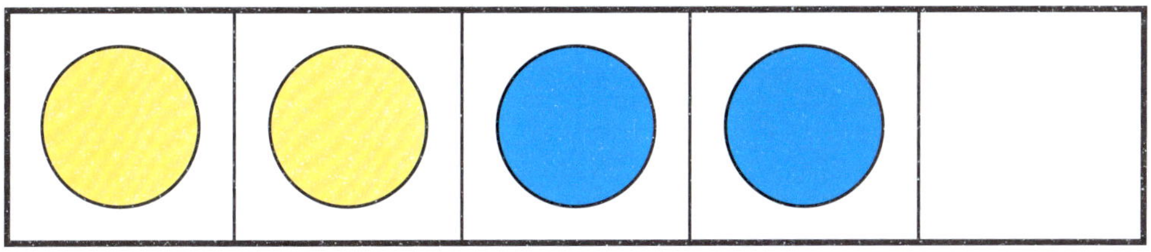

2 + 2 = ____

Got it! Not yet

You need:

I can join or combine a group of objects.

How many are there **in all**?
Write the number.
The first one is done for you.

1 + 2 = 3

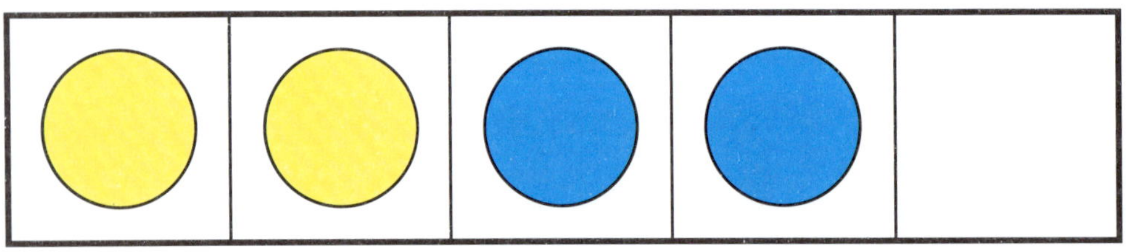

2 + 2 =

3 + 1 =

Got it! Not yet

I can join or combine a group of objects.

You need:

How many are there **in all**?
Write the number.

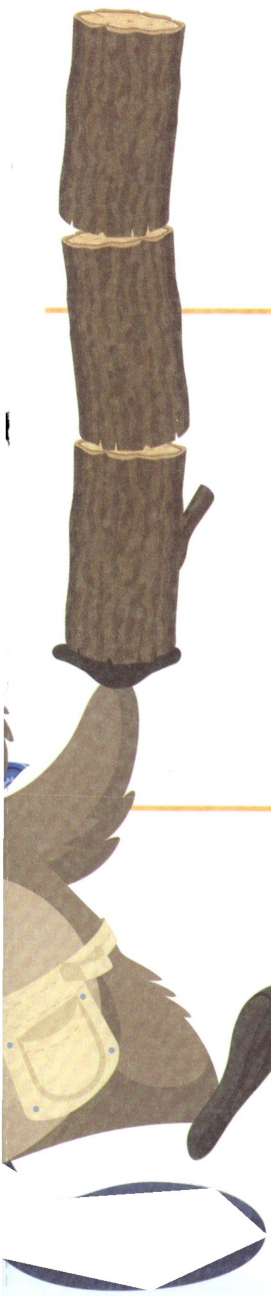

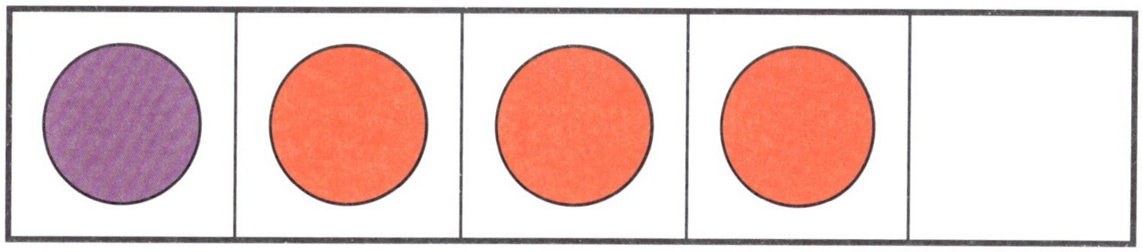

1 + 3 = ___

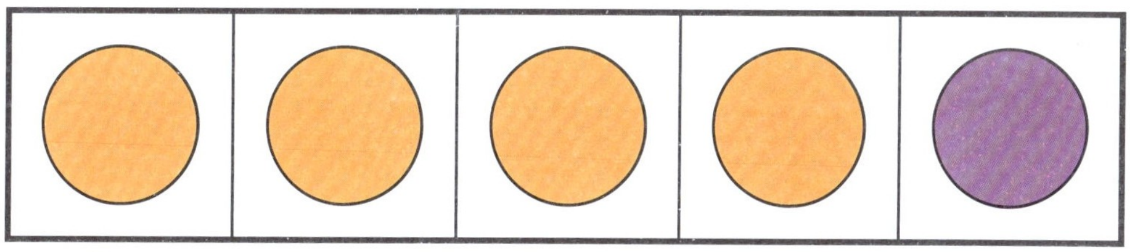

4 + 1 = ___

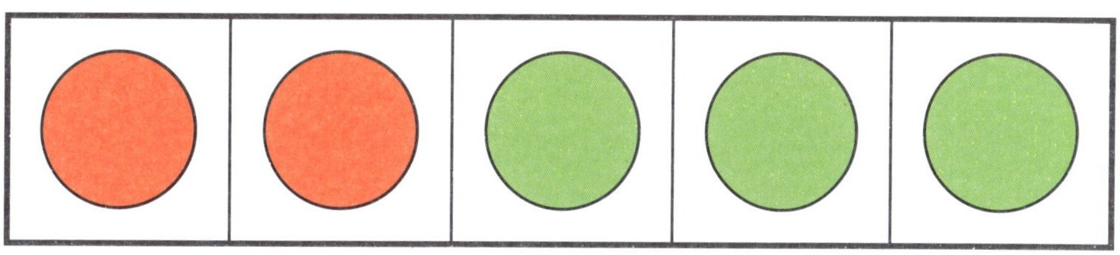

2 + 3 = ___

Got it! Not yet

I can use pictures and words to write.

(made-up stories, something that happened to me, to teach someone something)

Draw a picture to tell a story about something you love.
Label your picture.
Share your story with a family member.

Match the emotion.

You need:

Find and place the stickers to complete the scene.

Got it! Not yet

You need:

I can start to solve problems where I separate groups of objects.

How many are **left**?
Write the number.
The first one is done for you.

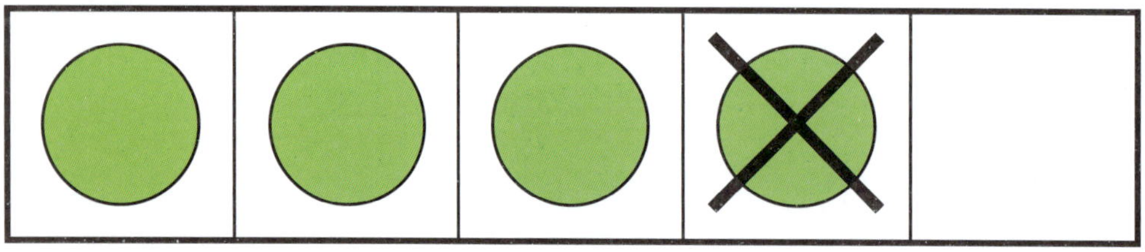

4 − 1 = 3

5 − 2 = ___

4 − 3 = ___

Got it! Not yet

You need:

I can start to solve problems where I separate groups of objects.

How many are **left**?
Write the number.

2 - 1 = ___

4 - 2 = ___

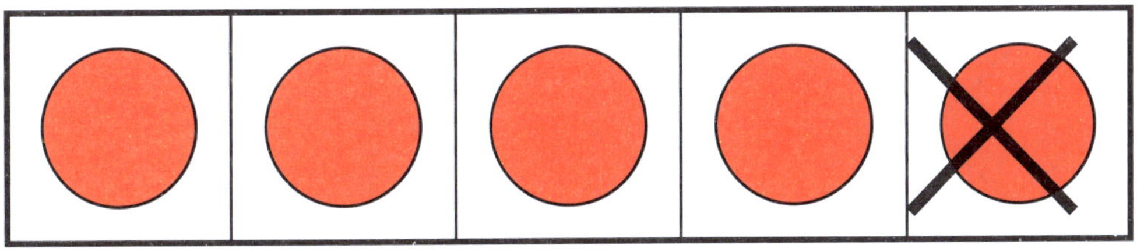

5 - 1 = ___

Got it! Not yet

I can start to solve problems where I separate groups of objects.

You need:

How many are **left**?
Write the number.

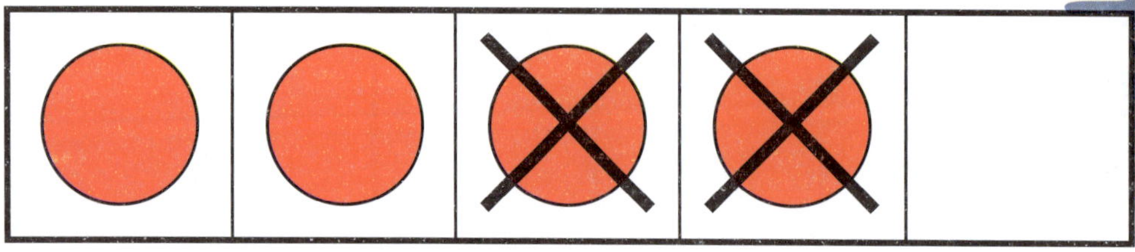

$4 - 2 =$ ____

$5 - 3 =$ ____

$3 - 1 =$ ____

Got it! Not yet

You need:

I can work in a group to write something together.

Make up a story with someone at home.
Draw a picture of the story together. Label your pictures.
You can both be the **author** and **illustrator**.

Parent Tip:
Ask your child what happened at the beginning of the story and what happened at the end of the story.

Got it! Not yet

I can estimate in my life.

You need:

An **estimate** is your best guess of how many things there are without counting.

Look at the first picture and **estimate** which group will fit into it. Circle the group.

Got it! Not yet

I can estimate in my life.

You need:

Look at the first picture and **estimate** which group will fit into it. Circle the group.

Got it! Not yet

Let's have some fun!

You need:

Circle what is different between **picture A** and **picture B**.

Picture A

Picture B

Got it! Not yet

Match the emotion.

You need:

Find and place the stickers to complete the scene.

Got it! Not yet

I can make my own book.

Below are instructions to cut out and assemble the book **All About Me**.

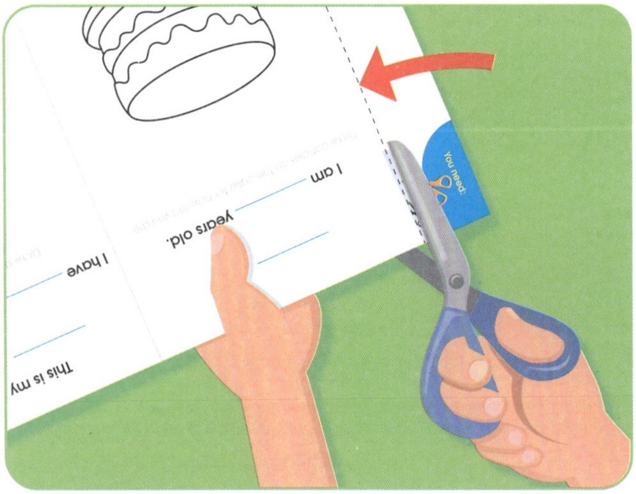

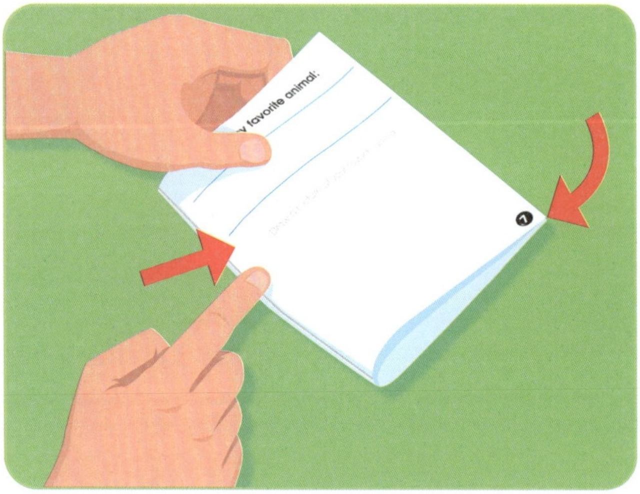

Step 1: Cut out the pages.
Use your scissors and carefully cut along the dotted lines to cut out the pages for the book.

Step 2: Fold the pages.
Take the pages you have just cut out and line up the left and right sides. Then press down on the center of the paper to make a crease along the gray line.

Step 3: Put the pages in order.
Place the folded pages in order from 1-12. The first page is the cover. The page numbers are on the bottom corner of each page.

Step 4: Fill in the pages.
Follow the directions for each page and write, draw, and color your book "**All About Me.**"

I can make my own book.

You need:

Cut out the book page on the dotted line.

Fold along gray line.

12

This book is
ALL ABOUT ME.
Who I am
and what I like.

ALL
ABOUT
ME

1

ALL ABOUT ME

Written by:

Illustrated by:

2

This is my favorite book:

Draw a picture from your favorite book.

11

I can make my own book.

You need:

Cut out the book page on the dotted line.

Fold along gray line.

4

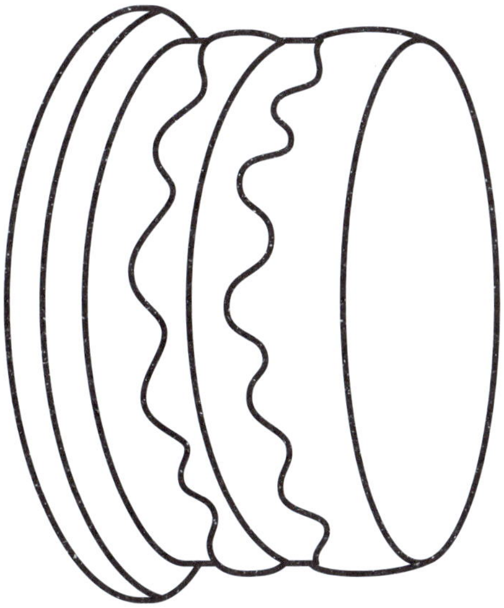

I am ______ years old.

Draw candles on the cake for how old you are.

This is my family:

I have ______ people in my family.

Draw a picture of your family.

6

This is where I live:

Draw a picture of where you live.

10

This is my name:

3

I can make my own book.

You need:

Cut out the book page on the dotted line.

Fold along gray line.

6

This is my favorite color:

Draw something that is your favorite color.

This is my favorite animal:

Draw a picture of your favorite animal.

7

This is my favorite food:

Draw a picture of your favorite food.

8

This is what I look like:

5